THE
RESILIENT
ORGANIZATION

THE
RESILIENT
ORGANIZATION
How Adaptive Cultures Thrive Even When Strategy Fails

LIISA VÄLIKANGAS

New York   Chicago   San Francisco
Lisbon   London   Madrid   Mexico City
Milan   New Delhi   San Juan   Seoul
Singapore   Sydney   Toronto

ISBN 978-0-07-166366-3
MHID 0-07-166366-5

McGraw-Hill books are available at special quantity discounts to use as premiums and sales promotions, or for use in corporate training programs. To contact a representative, please e-mail us at bulksales@mcgraw-hill.com.

This book is printed on acid-free paper.

To my father, Eero Välikangas

"'The time will come!' they said.
And waited with hope.
But when the time came, how many of them,
How many of them, were already gone."

—A. Minhajeva, Tatar Poet

Contents

Preface

A Note on Personal Resilience

The concepts of innovation and strategy have occupied me for a long time. Upon the conception of this book, many of the ideas expressed in various publications over the years came together in one overarching quest: Strategic Resilience! It represents the crucial capability to turn threats into opportunities before they become either, and it is a pursuit shared by strategists and innovators alike. Once threats emerge, it is often too late to do anything but desist and recover. And once explicit opportunities have taken shape, it is typically too late to lead.

What I mean by *strategic resilience* is somewhat different from the definition used in the abundant literature on recovery after a crisis, surviving trauma, or protecting against operational damage. The true art of strategic resilience is to wake up before such a crisis is upon us. Change *before* you have to (saving a great deal of money and pain). Turn threats into opportunities before they have time to form. The great advantage of such foresightedness is that it allows us the joy of discovery, experimentation, and innovation. Instead of saying, "Oh no, I have to do something before it is too late," we find ourselves saying, "Wow, that is cool. What next?"

I have spent the last 12 years in California's Silicon Valley, observing firsthand how such early opportunity creation takes place. This book builds on that experience, coupled with perspectives gained while working in Japan (early 1990s) and Switzerland (late 1980s). As a Finnish-Californian, I have a balanced view of resilience. The Finns emphasize stable endurance, in good times or bad—which is perhaps something that the Finns and the Japanese have in common—while the Californians, in my perception, rather revel in discovery and joy of life. Sure, these are archetypes and, as such, very rough and partially faulty descriptions. Nevertheless, the Finnish word for *resilience* is *sisu*, meaning tenacity, while the Californians admire "cool." I have tried to balance the two in this book: *strategic resilience* is both the ability to be selectively tenacious but also to engage fullheartedly and intensely in the joy of discovery.

As a professor in the Helsinki School of Economics (part of the new Aalto University in Finland), I have tried to convey this double-act to my students. Be coolly tenacious. As a frequent speaker on innovation to executive audiences, I have sought to explain the dual nature of innovation that so often frustrates managers. From the corporate point of view, I submit, innovation is too often viewed as merely a distraction—until it pays off. A busy workday is already so filled with urgent tasks that innovative ideas tend to get brushed off and pushed aside until the "real work" gets done. It is the capacity to entertain such distraction that will eventually pay off for a truly resilient company.

As a cofounder and president of a California-based nonprofit, Innovation Democracy, Inc., I have practiced extreme innovation (innovation in extreme conditions) together with Sari Stenfors of the Silicon Valley and Jaak Treiman of Los Angeles: supporting local innovation and entrepreneurship in countries such as Afghanistan that are important to world stability. Innovation Democracy specializes in making the impossible possible, one student and one venture at a time. Most recently, a number of our graduates visited the Silicon Valley and observed: "For us, this is like visiting Second Life," so different are the conditions in Afghanistan compared to those in the Silicon Valley. Innovation Democracy requires such resilience so that everyone's innovations can have their chance.

This book draws on my experiences in different spheres of life and work around the world. It is written to an audience of reflective practitioners and practice-inspired academics—people with whom I have conversed for a long time. Many of my colleagues are coauthors of the works included here. I very much appreciate your thoughtfulness, as well as the inspiration and joy that I have gained working with all of you.

The book offers a three-step strategy to creating a resilient organization. First, manage the consequences of past performance. Second, build resilience into the organization. Third, rehearse resilience enough so that it becomes second-nature so that your organization can thrive on resilience even when strategy, occasionally and inevitably, fails. The hardest part of this seemingly simple strategy—as I try to articulate in the cases, essays, and reflections in this book—is in the organizational effort at constantly working at resilience. If there are two kinds of problems in the world, those that are solved and those that are worked at, resilience definitely falls in the latter category.

My sincere hope is that you, the Reader, will find this book full of innovative and practical ideas, as well as managerial persuasions, from which to weave resilience. It is my personal mission to prove it's no longer true that "you can't be more wrong than to be right before your time." The imperative of strategic resilience is to be right before it is too late.

Today, more than ever, we need to be right before our time. As we face challenges to our environment, our organizations, and our very way of life, the time for strategic resilience has, once again, arrived.

WHY RESILIENCE NOW?

In 2003, the strategy professor and consultant Gary Hamel and I called for resilience to become a "quest" for corporations. We defined *resilience* as a capacity to undergo deep change without or prior to a crisis. Since then, enormous amounts of wealth have been lost in a global financial crisis. New urgency has been discovered regarding global warming with severe implications to our lifestyle. In 2003, we did not offer a managerial prescription guaranteed to "make" companies be resilient. This was to be a matter for management innovation. Rather than a how-to guide, our *Harvard Business Review* article, "The Quest for Resilience," was a clarion call for rethinking the principles and premises of management, so as to contrast and complement organizational hierarchy with a sense of initiative and community building. It was also a platform for developing the corresponding management practices that would make resilience an everyday habit rather than something to be grasped for only in the moment of crisis. These management practices would fill the *resilience gap*, defined as the world becoming turbulent faster than organizations are becoming resilient.

Such management innovation would help replace the "fallen eagles"—those presumptions of the past that got us into this mess. Perhaps the most famous such truth passé is evident in Alan Greenspan's shocking statement: "I made a mistake in presuming that the self-interest of organizations, specifically banks and others, was such that they were best capable of protecting their own shareholders and the equity." The implication is equivalent to the recognition of suicide bombers as a new security threat. No longer, it says, can the public interest be protected by relying on people's sense of self-preservation and their will to live (or make money).

I call these expired rules we have lived by the "fallen eagles." They worked once upon a time—some were even magnificent—but they fly no more.

FALLEN EAGLES

1. *Planning is sufficient preparation for the future.* Reality: Unknowable, extreme events make relying on plans questionable.
2. *Good strategy is key to success.* Reality: Most companies linger in a transition phase when the old strategy no longer works and the new one is yet to be fully implemented.
3. *People behave "rationally."* Reality: It is easy and commonplace to imitate other people's behavior or act out some fashionable idea rather than exercise independent judgment.
4. *Copying "best practices" cannot be argued against.* Reality: Untraditional competitors in emerging countries are right now redefining price/cost ratios and innovating new business models. Copying them is not possible—homegrown management innovation is needed.
5. *It is best to wait until change is absolutely necessary to save cost.* Reality: Such lack of rehearsal makes it extremely risky to accomplish change when the crisis is upon us.
6. *The art of management is about executing against preestablished goals and optimizing performance.* Reality: Discovering new aspirations and lifting performance horizons are current management priorities that require the cultivation of organization-wide innovation.
7. *Public interest can rely on organizational and/or individual self-interest and the imperative of self-preservation.* Reality: Public interest is, once again, for elected officials to guard. Such service will require highly qualified and altruistic people to govern. Citizens will need to become more active and informed too. High-quality journalism will be essential.
8. *We are masters of our ideas.* Reality: Ideas are powerful. They affect people's behavior, and they can now travel easily across places and people. We tend to believe that we own and use our ideas to our freely chosen ends, but actually, ideas tend to own us and manipulate our behavior toward their idea-driven ends. In the past decade, one such highly possessive idea has been the efficient market hypothesis.[1]

THE NEWLY FALLEN WORLD RISING: RESILIENCE REFORM

In the past, a call for resilience was an implied invitation, however persuasive, for crisis-free transformation. In contrast, today, as we are toddlering out of the deepest economic crisis since the 1930s' Depression, resilience has taken on an altogether new urgency, and the term must also gain new meaning. In this new world, *resilience* will again come to mean the capacity to survive the long term—not only its hardships but, more importantly perhaps, also the temptations to act for short-term benefit. Many an opportunity still looms. The question is how to pursue these opportunities, this time with resilience. We cannot and should not forgive ourselves for missing an opportunity for resilience reform—a rethink of what constitutes something worth building and something worth defending, fighting for—whether it is for our children and grandchildren or for our sense of life purpose and our consciousness. A reformation of the kind that took place in medieval Germany is needed: a rethink, not so much of what makes a good person (as per Martin Luther's theses) but what makes a good, resilient organization. Resilience principles need to replace the fallen eagles.

The past half-century, a period of extraordinary economic growth has exposed the frailties of our biological environment as never before, in a globally interconnected way. By 2020, or perhaps sooner, it will be impossible to reverse the devastating effects of global warming. The past decades of population and economic growth have simply been too taxing for our planet's powers of resilience. The very word *resilience* originates in part from ecological studies that measure it by assessing the disturbance that a system (in this case a particular natural environment) can absorb before it undergoes a major transformation [Hollnagel & Woods, 2006 (in Hollnagel, Woods, & Leveson, 2006)].

Iraq, the ancient Mesopotamia located between the rivers of Euphrates and Tigris, in addition to its difficulty in gaining peace, is suffering severe sandstorms due to draught and erosion of fertile land (*Los Angeles Times*,

July 30, 2009), and it may be turning into a wasteland. The citizens of the beautiful lagoon islands of the Maldives are looking for a new home as theirs may be swallowed by rising waters. A fire engulfing more than 100,000 square feet in its first week was burning the suburbs of Los Angeles at the end of August 2009. The LA firefighters called the fire "angry." In Europe, there has been a sharp rise in fatalities resulting from heat waves, such as the 2003 temperatures that killed 15,000 people in France alone. The planet evidently cannot sustain abusive wars, neglect, and rising temperatures without severe consequences to its capacity for sustaining life.

Even if the economy is turning around and a new growth period is now emerging, we should not let the crisis of the past years go to waste. It is an opportunity for transformation; but, more importantly, it is an opportunity also for reflection and learning. Indeed, it would be immoral and wasteful not to take the opportunity to learn.

RESISTANCE OR ADAPTATION?

When the ecologists talk about "resilience," they mean the ability of a system to resist major change (or, to endure perturbances without systemic change). When population ecologists in business schools talk about "structural inertia," they consider it a hallmark of stability and reliability in a company. This forms the absorptive fodder that ideally eliminates the need for restructuring. When Gary Hamel and I wrote about resilience in 2003 in the corporate context, we assumed that change is necessary and that, rather than focus on resistance, it would be best to focus on cost: how to effect change as cheaply, or as free of trauma, as possible. Figure 1.1 presents this simple framework: any change can be evaluated relative to its cost.

Cheap change might mean small-scale experimentation that, if it works, is eventually scaled up. It might also mean the compounding of many experiments so that they add up to something significant. Or it might mean learning from others because doing so is presumably cheaper than going through the experience and inevitable failures yourself. Change that comes cheap might also mean starting early, so that there is time for learning and correction while all options are still open—no need to take potentially huge, costly, traumatic, and life-changing risks.

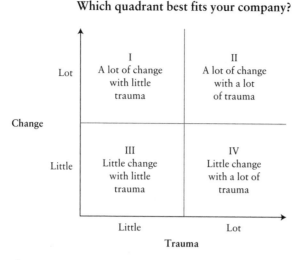

Figure 1.1 Change versus Cost (Trauma)

PLATFORMS FOR TRAUMA-FREE CHANGE

- Play extends reality into an imaginary universe.
- Experimentation allows failure that is natural, an opportunity for learning, and thus does not carry a stigma.
- Imagination substitutes for real action (and thus takes away risk).
- Reading history and fictional stories teaches lessons without having to experience it all oneself.
- Prototyping offers a way to make proposals concrete.
- Building "innovation rag dolls" (rough physical representations) enables play with innovation ideas.
- Virtual games and virtual worlds offer exploratory environments for collective behaviors.

Most projects can be designed to contain risk while experimenting on the new by their nature of being limited in time, scope, and budget. However, the history of management is a history of delay: incumbent corporations have found it phenomenally difficult to accomplish change absent a forcing function such as a financial crisis (Hamel & Välikangas, 2003).

Even when management is painfully aware of the need for change, the corporation is still often unable to accomplish it. General Motors now wishes to bring its newly found sense of urgency of going through bankruptcy in 40 days to the new GM (*Washington Post*, July 10, 2009). The delay in transforming itself into a presumably viable company came at a cost of $50 billion in taxpayer money. But many highly successful companies often face the same issue: they cannot reform their operations while they are still performing relatively well. The engine cannot be changed in midflight. The whole flight plan must be canceled before serious change becomes possible.

Concrete, short-term urgencies override the long-term, and usually abstract, need for renewal. A lot of management excellence–motivated ink has been spilled over the balancing of exploitation of the present (earning revenue) with exploration for the future (building future business), and there's still much more to come. However, rather than using this book to try to overturn the old truth that "one bird in the hand is better than two in the bush," I suggest we accept the difficulty of transition and acknowledge its typically delayed nature despite calls for creative destruction (how to cannibalize your business now), strategic innovation (compete for the future), or the innovator's solution (which stems from the innovator's paradox—doing well for today makes it difficult to adjust to the future). We should not forget the risks either: a strong-headed pursuit of the unknown is probably good for humankind (we get to learn) but not so good for the adventurers who eventually pay the price. Niccolò Machiavelli (1469–1527) already noted that "the benefits to the innovator are uncertain, but the costs to those affected by the changes involved are not."

In the spirit of the Reaganesque "trust but verify," let us not abandon our efforts to reinvent the future (this is the "trust" component), but let us also survive until the future we work for is here (thus we "verify" the claimed progress). Luft and Korin [2007: 81 (in Fukuyama, 2007)] suggest a great need to move from "an oil-based economy to a fuel-choice economy," but they admit that the move will take time. The question is: What shall we do in the meanwhile, while this transition slowly rolls along, recovering from many erroneous moves and dead-end paths?

Let us build resilience—to close the gap between the future and our capability to meet it.

FALLEN EAGLES: BET ON RESILIENCE, NOT ON STRATEGY

Simply stated: While most authors and executives are busy trying to hit upon a strategy for success and then forging its perpetuation, I propose that a more reasonable preoccupation would be building corporate resilience amid times of extreme uncertainty, especially when you consider the poor record of strategies actually delivering their (full) promise (see, for example, "Pop! Went the Profit Bubble," *Fortune*, May 4, 2009;[1] also Campbell-Hunt, 2000). Resilience is the capacity that sustains the business while the strategists are hard at work. It is also the capacity to survive rare events—unexpected changes that may be minor (like Apple's iPod) or major (the 2008 financial crisis). When something unexpected happens, or our assumptions about likelihoods, causal sequences, and human behavior turn out wrong, it is resilience we fall back on.

It is difficult to evaluate the quality of strategy independently of its performance. Can a strategy be "good" despite performing poorly? A CEO can believe in a strategy that has yet to deliver, but will the investors? Using performance as a guide to the goodness or fitness of a particular strategy easily becomes a tautology. Beyond current performance, a company is as resilient as its ability to survive and thrive over multiple major changes in its competitive environment. Being resilient means taking a longer-term perspective.

Most of strategy literature focuses on how to arrive at a winning strategy. This may require superior customer insight, leadership agility, innovativeness, or good execution. Yet the record of success through strategy excellence leaves enough failures to suggest that wise and responsible corporate leadership should not focus on strategy formulation and implementation alone (for example, Witteloostuijn, 1998). In other words, don't bet the company on its current strategy. Rather, consider two other factors as well.

First, companies need to look at how they manage when strategy is not yet or no longer performing optimally. Resilience provides the capacity to sustain strategy change. It is the strength an organization draws on in the in-between state, when the old strategy is not really working and the new one is still being developed. What we need to realize is that this in-between-strategies state is now the dominant mode in most companies! Nokia is seeking to reinvent itself as a software and services company (it is no longer device focused, though it launched its first notebook, a new device for the Internet). Microsoft is trying to become an Internet company. General Electric is seeking rapidly to lessen its dependence on its financial business and become an imaginative "green" company. British Petroleum was, until recently, poised to become a company focused on alternative technologies ("beyond petroleum"). The Finnish paper company UPM is becoming an energy company. Amazon.com has long been moving toward becoming an Internet marketplace in which many other product lines in addition to books are sold. And Starbucks is seeking to return to its roots as a great coffee company. The prevalence of such frequent transitory states emphasizes the importance of resilience—the company's carrying force throughout change.

Second, a lot of strategy literature suggests that great companies fail not because of something they *don't* do but because of something they do *too much*: they cannot stop.

Polaroid did not manage to transition from instant photography and film into digital cameras, despite its having invested in relevant R&D and making other preparatory moves in digital technology. The company simply could not give up its heritage in instant film. (Even now, there is an admirable movement to rejuvenate the old instant photography technology by Polaroid employees and hobbyists together, as reported by the *Financial Times*, August 15, 2009. The "Impossible Project" has drawn modest investment, but its real mission is "to release new stocks of film before the last supplies expire" to prevent camera owners' trashing their cameras before they will be able to get new film.)

Many companies, just like Polaroid, keep doing what they did well in the past, long after it is of any commercial value or market relevance—this is the so-called Icarus Paradox identified by Danny Miller (1990). Resilience—in this sense, tenacity—may help a company to survive far beyond when its strategy has lost all vitality. It would take a long time, for example, for Microsoft—a very asset rich company—to burn down all of its accumulated billion-dollar wealth during times of its great success as a PC software powerhouse, even if the company stopped producing new success stories. Companies like Microsoft may be "permanently failing" for a long time before they go bankrupt (Meyer & Zucker, 1989). The hard question is—as Jim Collins poses in his book *How the Mighty Fall:* how would we know (or rather, be convinced) we are failing when our performance is still technically acceptable?

THE DEMISE OF STRATEGY AND ITS DELAYED SUCCESS

In addition to the difficulty of being flexible in strategy implementation once it is formulated or giving up a strategy when it's no longer working, there are two conceptual strikes that can be made against strategy.

First, we don't have a very accurate model of how the world (generally, on a normal day) works. The recent fall of financial economics is a perfect illustration of this point. The reality did not follow theoretical predictions, nor risk assessments. Triana (2008: 20), in a spirited critique, has stated that Bear Stearns' Value-at-Risk, a common measure in the financial industry of a company's possible loss at the end of the trading day, was $60 million just a few days prior to failure (with declared assets worth $8 billion). Further, Gillian Tett, in the *Financial Times* (July 24, 2009: 18), has suggested that not only are there uncertain expectations as to whether inflation or deflation is to result from the "quantitative easing" practices by the Federal Reserve in the United States in 2009, but there is also confusion as to the very intellectual framework that would help answer the question. "The old economic models . . . no longer look reliable."

Furthermore, Nassim Nicholas Taleb (2007: xx) persuades us forcefully that we do not even know that we do not know (or conversely, what we know does not really help us much): "The inability to predict outliers implies the inability to predict the course of history. . . . What is surprising is not the magnitude of our forecast errors, *but our absence of awareness of it*" (italics added). In part, the knowledge we have (provided that others know we have it) prevents such outlier events from happening, at least if they are human intended.

There is fundamental uncertainty about future prospects. The future is unknowable. On which, then, do we build our strategies?

Second, there are a number of extraordinary events that disturb the assumed normalcy. Taleb (2007), again, writes about rare, potentially catastrophic events that he calls "black swans," whose occurrences cannot be predicted in time. Bill McKelvey, a professor at UCLA's Anderson School of Management, has strongly criticized the use of normal distribution as a basis for organizational theorizing. He has suggested that the power law distribution—an expression of probabilities frequent in networks—is a much more accurate basis for study when there is connectivity. Power law distributions have long tails, suggesting that they do not behave the way that events do according to normal distribution. It is not only that people are "boundedly rational" (Simon, 1979) or that biases and decision-making heuristics distort the choice toward less "rational" or theoretically optimal outcomes (Kahneman & Tversky, 1979). It is also that risks, in rare instances, may become highly correlated even if they have shown independence in the past. It is a sort of domino effect, a collapse of past tendencies into one big meltdown. The world has become so interconnected that everything now depends on everything else: banks don't lend, organizations run out of money, people stop buying, there are no jobs. There is no market to buy and sell.

A potential third strike against strategy is the temptation for ruling by hindsight. Professor Karl Weick at the University of Michigan is attributed a saying akin to "Strategy is sense making in retrospect." The realized outcome looks inevitable only now that we know which dots to connect and which to ignore. Naturally, looking forward we see potential for a multitude of possibilities. Honda's entry to the U.S. car market is perhaps the most often told story of retrospective strategizing (see Pascale, 1984, 1996). The Honda representatives discovered the demand for small motorcycles by accident. ("An old lady asked where to buy a motorbike like the one the Honda representative was driving.") Reluctant to dilute their brand image as a maker of great cars with small motorcycles, and acting without the knowledge of corporate management, the Honda representatives nevertheless decided that selling motorcycles was their only option, having failed to achieve straightforward U.S. market entry earlier with automobiles. In retrospect, Honda appeared to have executed a brilliant strategy (see the BCG report *Strategy Alternatives for the British Motorcycle Industry*, 1973). Similarly, Best Buy, a highly successful U.S. consumer electronics retailer, saw the beginning of its big-box retailing in electronics in a Midwestern tornado that caused water damage to the inventory. Discounted electronics were a hit, and thereby a business model was born. Serendipity, rather than strategy, was the true force at work.

Strategy has been the bulwark against uncertainty, on one hand, and the magic wand for success on the other. [Think of "blue ocean strategies" by Kim and Mauborgne (2005), for example, where the focus is on the discovery of the heretofore "uncompeted" business arenas.] Perhaps only the word *innovation* is more reliable than *strategy* for lifting spirits toward victory. Yet strategy has diminished in stature due to its proven inability to cope with fundamental shifts in the business environment. "No visibility" was the expression used by the CEO John Chambers of Cisco Systems in the dot-com bust of the 2000. "Impossible to call" say many more executives in 2009, though the Nokia CEO Olli-Pekka Kallasvuo claimed "the freefall" had ended in late spring 2009. Indeed, even in the best times, the role of strategy is unclear: "The market was growing so fast there was no need for strategy" was one executive's explanation of his company's process in the late 1990s. Just crank those phones out, efficiently and reliably. No wonder Nokia's strongest suit is logistics (Arlbjorn et al., 2008).

Rarely is there only one way to see a situation. Some people would claim that Nokia's success was due to an agile strategy (Doz & Kosonen, 2008); others would suggest it was being in the right place at the right time: the company benefited from a long-term investment in radio technology; the free markets in telephony in Finland; the Nordic GSM standard; the rise from a deep recession that created a sort of "winter war mentality" (Finnish for a determination to win); the support of the state in R&D; and the rapid expansion of education of electrical engineers in Finland (see Lovio, 1993). Such ambiguity is both the demise and the promise of strategy. That there is room for imagination and insight, serendipity, and luck, as well as determination, leaves a good strategist an opening. However, heat-of-the-moment decisions often form a (coherent) strategy only in retrospect.

THE DELAYED SUCCESS OF STRATEGY

Strategy can be understood and practiced as a targeted process of discovery. In this sense, strategy is meant to both shape and interpret the future. For such discovery to be helpful, it has to be fast enough to keep up with the changes in the competitive environment and lucky enough in its exploration to turn up something strategically worthwhile. The discovery must also be true to the emerging market opportunities.

Too often, an eventual discovery threatens the existing business model, which makes the discovery difficult to pursue as a business opportunity—not always because of arrogance or complacency; usually for much more mundane reasons.

Daily agendas are already full. It is difficult to change routine behaviors that sustain the old business models and are cemented in organizational hierarchy and structures. Doing something out of the ordinary risks embarrassment and rejection. There are many good reasons—temptations, even—to continue as before.

Thus the need for the core resilience of the corporation—while waiting for the eventual success of the strategy in discovery, then in formulation, and finally in implementation, to overcome the often persistent commitment to the past. GE, for example, needs such resilience in its current transition. A preeminent U.S. company, it is in the process of reinventing itself once more: as an imaginative, sustainable, organic growth company. Amazon.com has been highly resilient in pursuing its long-term strategy. Jeff Bezos, its CEO, has often stated that Amazon.com will stay the course, despite short-term challenges, toward becoming the premier customer-focused service site on the Internet. Bezos does not waiver in his commitment. In a *Business Week* interview (April 17, 2008), he recalled: "I remember one meeting where one of our executives said to me, 'So how much are you prepared to spend on Kindle, anyway?' I looked at him and said, 'How much do we have?'"

VOICE OF RESILIENCE

Amazon.com acquired the online shoe retailer Zappos in July 2009. The *New York Times* reported (July 22, 2009) that the management team of Zappos would remain intact. Zappos has a favorable reputation among consumers owing to its personalized service, free overnight shipping, and its policy of allowing buyers to return any pair of shoes free. "We plan to continue to run Zappos the way we have always run Zappos—continuing to do what we believe is best for our brand, our culture, and our business," wrote Tony Hsieh, the Zappos CEO. Jeff Bezos, Amazon.com's chief executive, praised Zappos as having "a customer obsession, which is so easy for me to admire. . . . I get all weak-kneed when I see a customer-obsessed company."

TOWARD RESILIENCE

Historically, we have tended to think of resilience as a fallback. Resilience has typically been seen as an ability to bounce back after strategy failure, to make a recovery, or to persist during a crisis. Table 2.1 contrasts this notion of resilience as a crisis capability (Resilience II) to our new proposed notion of resilience that begins by taking timely action *before* the misfortune has a chance to wreak havoc (Resilience I).

Table 2.1   Conceptions of Resilience

Resilience I The capacity to:	Resilience II The capacity to:
• Change without first experiencing a crisis	• Recover after experiencing a crisis
• Change without a lot of accompanying trauma	• Persist in the face of threat; not to yield; tenacity
• Take action before it is a final necessity	• Survive trauma

---

EXAMPLES OF RESILIENCE I AND II

The United States showed great resilience after 9/11. The economic recovery, after the most serious attack in U.S. history, was remarkable, and the people's collective determination not to give in to terrorism was laudable. This was Resilience II. However, in terms of Resilience I, the record is less admirable. Despite multiple indications of a possible terrorist threat, no preventative action was taken. The *9/11 Commission Report* calls the events "a shock, not a surprise" (see the Executive Summary, p. 2). Further, the eventual response to the threat—the formation of a large Homeland Security Department—is questionable in terms of its ability to meet an ever-changing variety of threats. The formation of a prison camp in Guantanamo Bay also marked a forfeiture of the very values the country was supposed to defend, thus opening up an opportunity for the enemy to cry hypocrisy. All these things diminish Resilience I, the capacity to turn the threat—hostile action—into an opportunity, namely the beginning of a new kind of relationship between the peoples of the United States and the Middle East (something President Obama attempted in his speech in Cairo, June 4, 2009).

I define *strategic resilience* as *the capability to turn threats into opportunities prior to their becoming either*. This is a definition closer to Resilience I than Resilience II, but it sets an even higher standard. It is not sufficient to momentarily neutralize (Resilience I) or survive (Resilience II) threats—in the long term, such threats tend to resurface and wear the company down.

Foundational to such resilience is having the courage to *see* opportunity where others see threat. Vinod Khosla, a highly acclaimed venture capitalist in the Silicon Valley, recently raised $1.1 billion "to spur development of renewable energy and other clean technologies" (*Los Angeles Times*, September 2, 2009). Khosla describes part of the funding as "science experiments," which perfectly captures the potential for serendipity—to create positive surprises, insightful understandings, or framings of happenstance events—that is so critical for resilience. These kinds of surprises are "fat tail" (rare) events that are outside the normal course of operations. They could turn in a nasty direction, but a resilient company is able instead to turn these surprises to its advantage. A resilient company is alert and poised enough to see the irregularity, and it is also conscious enough to make sense of it.

Thus resilience is not about having a highly competitive strategy or executing it faithfully. Rather, it's about the company's capacity to benefit from unlikely events, which could have been threats, and turning them into opportunities. It's about the capacity to take advantage of serendipity—to be "accidentally sagacious" like the Princes of Serendip, who in Robert Merton and Elinor Barber's 2004 book *The Travels and Adventures of Serendipity*, traveled the world and smartly found opportunity to learn something they were not originally seeking:

> "As their Highnesses traveled, they were always making discoveries, by accidents and sagacity, of things which they were not in the quest of: for instance, one of them discovered that a mule blind of the right eye had traveled in the same road lately, because the grass was eaten only on the left side, where it was worse than on the right—now do you understand *Serendipity*?" (pp. 1–2)

TRAVELS OF SERENDIPITY

The discovery of the new and unexpected is often *serendipitous*—it happens without intentional search for the particular happenstance but being alert and tuned in enough to take note. The letter of January 28, 1754, to Horace Mann by Horace Walpole, the original serendipity storyteller (Merton & Barber, 2004), states that such "accidental sagacity" excludes any "discovery of a thing you are looking for." Yet as the story defines, such luck requires "sagacity" to see and interpret what one may have encountered. As the luck favors the prepared, similarly serendipity is likely to inhabit those who take an active interest in their surroundings, engage with discovery, and have the capacity to interpret and seize the potential importance of serendipitous events as they occur. This amounts to sagacity, a particular kind of alert wisdom.

To the extent that corporate strategy encourages and supports such accidental sagacity, it can be said to have resilience value:

$$\text{Resilience} = \text{Serendipity} + \text{Sagacity}$$

Unfortunately, there is no set formula for doing that. The steps described in this book—managing the consequences of past performance, building resilience into the organization, and rehearsing the culture of resilience—will help and provide a platform for resilience. Yet to truly turn threats into opportunities, you also need a good story, like the Honda story, which is still being told and is very specific to that company—that is, a story that can be generalized. (How would you find the appropriate old lady when needed?) Thus building a simplistic theory on how to get to resilience is likely to be of no help. There are elements that must be present, such as an internal champion, resources, and timing. Yet the *presence of these elements does not necessarily make it happen.* Crucial as they may be, they do not yet breathe life into the situation. Turning threats into opportunities requires business savvy—the lifeline of successful venturing. This is why a lot of theory on innovation is stillborn—consisting of prescriptive steps that are formulated post hoc, eminently reasonable but lacking creative power.

The strategic resilience definition—turning threats into opportunities before their becoming either—has a number of prerequisites. Not all situations require or can benefit from such resilience. Here are some factors that encourage it:

1. The environment lacks constancy. There is a lot of dynamism or turbulence, that is, potential for interactions with threat-opportunities. (Should there be constancy, mere organizational stability suffices.)
2. The organization is strategically evolvable; that is, it is capable of innovation and change.
3. There is strategic intent or poisedness; therefore, the organization is not simply a passive object for environmental perturbations, but instead, it exercises choice as to which threat-opportunities to respond to and how. (Some threat-opportunities may not be worth bothering with; responses to others may close out future options; and so on.)

4. The organization is able to take timely action. (By the time a threat emerges, it is often too late to turn it into an opportunity.)

Succeeding at resilience, as defined above, requires not simplistic formulas but business savvy.

In *Resilience Engineering*, Hollnagel and Woods (2006: 356–357) talk about the importance of viewing surprises not as failures of analysis but as opportunities for learning and adaptation. They write, for example: "If 'surprises' are seen as recognition of the need constantly to update definitions of the difference between success and failure, then inquiry centers on the kinds of variations which our systems should be able to handle and ways constantly to test the system's ability to handle these classes of variations."

PARTS MORE RESILIENT THAN THE WHOLE

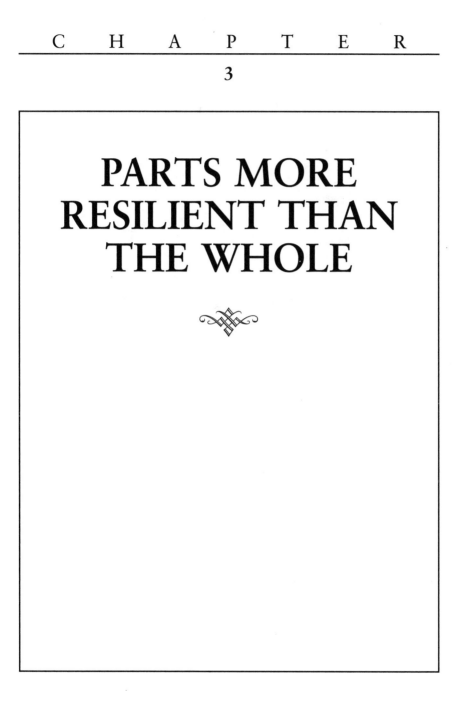

Now, what is resilient? Or, asked differently, what is the unit of resilience?

Richard Dawkins (1976, 2006) claims that genes are actually more resilient than people. They recombine with others. They mutate. They evolve. They are subject to natural selection (and hence test their resilience; no time for complacency). They benefit from serendipity if there is an appropriate "preadaptation" or mutation present. There is redundancy as insurance. In these qualities, genes speak to the innate resilience that life manifests.

Dawkins's formative thinking has been extended to memes—units of cultural expression, such as ideas like capitalism or rituals like handshaking—that spread through mimicry or imitation. The discussion is insightful in its suggestion of a *unit* that is particularly resilient—not people, organizations, or nations but, like atoms, the much smaller building blocks of life and/or culture. Let's look at one of our most recent microunits, the *tweet*:

ARE TWEETS RESILIENT?

"What are you doing now?" The microblogging service that invites people to send messages of fewer than 140 characters in response to this question has some 3 million users, of whom 200,000 are active on a daily basis (Comm, 2009: 4). However, the users are very fragmented in terms of whose message streams they follow. A recent survey (*Fast Company*, July/August 2009) reported that 24 percent of Twitter users had between 11 and 25 followers. According to Joel Comm, "The top 10 percent of Twitterers have more than [or only!—ed note] 80 followers and follow more than 70 people." The tweet universe is then highly

---

(*continued*)

distributed, with some 4 million connections among users. Tweets may be the new unit of communication that—like genes and memes—are highly resilient, more so than books, articles, news releases, or other more complete, *and less mobile*, means of communication.

Source: www.fastcompany.com/blog/cheryl-contee/fission-strategy/new-studies-provide-insight-twitter-tweeters (July 31, 2009).

The key to resilience according to nature is to make the parts more resilient than the whole. To accomplish this feat, the parts—the genes and memes and tweets—need to be able to combine with others (there are many more gene combinations available than atoms in the known universe); be variative in their expressions (thus not be of any one kind); be constantly tested through competition for survival; mutate (and hence be beneficent of serendipity); and finally, be able to travel (Czarniawska & Joerges, 1996; Czarniawska & Sevón, 2005). They must interact with other genes and memes in different locations, in different parts of the world, virtually or physically. The benefit is to be exposed to different influences and thus avoid orthodoxy (in the case of memes) and incest (in the case of genes).

RESILIENCE CHARACTERISTICS

- Redundant (insurance for failure or error)
- Recombinatory (not monolithic)
- Variative (mutating)
- Subject to natural selection or resilience test (not complacent)
- Subject to and/or beneficiary of serendipity (not isolated, capacity to benefit from luck)
- Mobile (able to interact across distance)

Genes may be more resilient than individuals, but individuals tend to be more resilient than large corporations, which live, on average, shorter lives than people do (about 40 or so years). Charles D. Ellis's account of Goldman Sachs mostly recounts the contributions of the remarkable individuals who built it. Its early leaders Sidney Weinberg, Gus Levy, and others understood the importance of connections in addition to hard work, and they did not look down on some occasional ruthlessness and credit taking. They were highly resilient individuals, and their resilience spilled over to their company. Indeed, the Sachs family even stepped aside to let Sidney Weinberg lead the firm back from its Depression disaster: "['The Brooklyn boy' Weinberg] was smarter and tougher than [the genteel Sachses] were, and [the Sachses] could not do what had to be done" (Ellis, 2008: 31). Perhaps due to the constitutive efforts of these early entrepreneurs (and later statesmen), Goldman Sachs today shows resilience as a company, emerging strong from the 2008 to 2009 financial crisis. They developed the company's capability to be resilient—turning threats such as a financial crisis into growth opportunities. (In March 2009, in the midst of the global financial turmoil, Goldman Sachs reported a much stronger than expected quarterly profit of $1.8 billion.)

THE ROLE OF OPERATIONAL RESILIENCE

Let us note the established literature on *operational resilience*, which studies the capacity of an organization to sustain threat and accomplish accident recovery (or avoid accidents in the first place). It is largely a defensive capability, and it stems from the tradition of engineering (Hollnagel, Woods, & Leveson, 2006). This tradition has sought to build systems that are robust despite perturbations (that is, systems that don't change when circumstances change). Related management literature proposes *organizational qualities* (such as mindfulness) that are crucial for such safety performance. Weick and Sutcliffe (2007) write about the lessons of highly reliable organizations: good management practices that apply generally but especially in the face of unexpected events or emergencies.

Operational resilience is about *not* succumbing to such discrete events that will—like California earthquakes—inevitably happen, sooner or later, bigger or smaller. Operational resilience is also about avoiding human error—being extra careful in operating the nuclear plant, for example, despite the evidence that accidents are to some extent part of the normal life in organizations (Perrow, 1984, 1986) and therefore must be expected. This

important stream of research considers accidents not abnormalities of organizational life but natural accompaniments to the complexity that organizations inevitably manifest and create. This literature is related to the studies of accidents that view them as eventual (difficult to avoid) endpoints of
chains of escalating events (for example, Vaughan, 1996; Hänninen, 2007;
Allison, 1971).

Operational Resilience	Strategic Resilience
Accident avoidance and recovery	Capacity to sustain and accomplish strategy change
Mindfulness	Capacity to create positive surprises
Robustness	Sustainability
	Escalation avoidance

In sum, operational resilience is the antidote for a sudden shock or jolt.
It is the strength or stability that is needed in case of such a sudden disturbance. However, a broader kind of resilience is needed to combat long-last-
ing organizational decline: strategic resilience. In the spirit of Karl Weick's
"safety is a nondynamic event" (see Hollnagel & Woods, 2006), strategic
resilience is what dynamically prevents the organization from falling into
decline, thus ensuring that a crisis never comes. Strategic resilience, as
earlier noted, is also a capacity to exploit an (imminent or long-term)
opportunity.

Threats	Responses
Disturbance (sudden)	Operational resilience
Decline (long-lasting)	Strategic resilience
Opportunity (imminent or long term)	Strategic resilience

There are a number of reasons corporations struggle to adapt to new market realities. Like Polaroid, their strategies may be obsolete and not engaged with the needs and desires of the market anymore. Commitment may be escalating to an irreversible course of action that turns out to be risky (John F. Kennedy's Bay of Pigs—an embarrassing overture to Cuba) or costly (losing lives as in the war in Iraq). Management may be malfunctioning, lacking the fortitude to lead effectively (like the state of California's budget negotiations). Structural inertia in the form of established organizational structures (such as business units that operate as silos) and rigid operating processes may prevent any change from taking hold. There may be (relative) incompetence—an industry-regulating body may be at a relative disadvantage compared to an investment bank when it comes to recruiting the best and brightest, for example.

More dynamic explanations suggest that under severe threat, an organization is likely to resort to well-rehearsed routine behaviors, even if they are totally inappropriate to the emergent situation. For example, it is easy to resort to cutting costs when what's really needed is a new product innovation. There are also a number of performance traps that companies may fall into myopically. *Failure traps* occur when the organization lacks the patience to wait and see if a particular strategy works, and thus keeps changing the strategy prematurely (Levinthal & March, 1993). *Success traps* are the seductive consequences of overconfidence and hubris, or simply continuing to do what the organization does well until it is no longer relevant to the changed market realities.

In the article "Boundary-Setting Strategies for Escaping Innovation Traps," with Michael Gibbert in the *MIT Sloan Management Review* in 2005, I discussed performance, commitment, and business model traps as antecedents of the lack of innovation and hence ultimately the lack of resilience. The performance issue has been discussed above as *success and failure traps*. The *commitment trap* results either from continuous experimentation where no commitment can be produced or maintained to a particular course of action (a sort of weakness-of-will situation) or from excessive self-confidence that leads to a belief in a particular Big Opportunity that is not adequately understood or prepared as a business opportunity. The *business model trap* follows the neglect of the signals of change in the environment or the forcing of emergent innovation to conform to the existing business model, thus negating its uniqueness or novel potential.

ORGANIZATIONAL DECLINE

Factors Underlying the Inability to Accomplish Strategy Change

- Strategic obsolescence
- Escalating commitment (to an undesirable course of action)
- Strategic drift
- Management malfunctioning
- Structural inertia
- Incompetence
- Threat-rigidity effect
- Success and/or failure traps

CONSIDER SUSTAINABILITY

In addition to being strategically resilient, another related challenge is worth naming. *Sustainability* takes a different view of the challenge of long-term survival. It is about the benevolence of the environment toward the company. It is about the company's amount of vested goodwill, legitimacy, and friends in the environment it shares. Apple is a good example of a company that has earned so much customer dedication that it is as much a movement as a corporation; it could ask its army of followers to do almost anything and succeed—a huge boon to its future prospects.

How to make the organization more sustainable? This requires thinking of the company and its community as being a common unit with shared interests, risks, and goals. Rather than fighting to win at the expense of others' well-being, sustainability requires actions that acknowledge and seek to improve the shared fate and the joint lot. For example, as is well known, open source software practices expect any code improvement (or problem solved) to be contributed to the benefit of all users as a precondition to accessing the source code. Sustainability and resilience are related in that they both seek to improve long-term prospects; sustainability by making choices that lessen the burden the environment must bear, and resilience by developing capacity to make timely changes before they become too costly.

THE TESTS OF RESILIENCE

Resilience has a number of tests it must choose from to prove itself. A shielded life suggests privilege, not resilience. Even a long life in itself might not suggest resilience—for instance, an organization living off an uncontested natural resource might not be resilient at all. Nevertheless, longevity is certainly worth something—if only the chance to learn through experience. (However, the paradox of resilience is that strategic resilience really means learning by means other than crisis- or failure-taught experience.) In this sense, resilience is about learning *without* having to learn from experience.

Competition

The first and most obvious external test of resilience is competition. Those that survive a competitive threat are by definition found resilient at a point in time (that of the testing).

Competitive logic invites a contest for superior know-how or resource use to produce something that the judge (such as the paying customer) perceives to be of value. Traditionally, (non)competitive strategies have been divided into those that focus on superior quality (differentiation) and those that produce the lowest cost (price competitiveness). The basis for such strategies may be, for example, a unique customer insight, superior managerial competence, or control of some rare resource, an entry barrier, or certain intellectual property. Upstarts may disrupt the landscape, but occasionally, as in the case of proprietary technology like Microsoft's Windows or a natural resource like oil, users develop a dependency that becomes a source of power for the producers. Such complacency can be exploited for premium pricing. These types of strategies exploit market dominance and are hence, by nature, noncompetitive: dominant power can be used for good or for bad, but eventually, without competition, it is said to corrupt. Buyer beware.

An example of a strategy based on resource control is a statement that was made by Condoleezza Rice, former secretary of state. According to Luft and Korin [2007: 75–76 (in Fukuyama, 2007)], Secretary Rice said the following to the Senate Foreign Relations Committee in 2006:

> We do have to do something about the energy problem. I can tell you that nothing has really taken me aback more, as secretary of state, than the way the politics of energy is . . . "warping" diplomacy around the world. It has given extraordinary powers to some states that are using that power in not very good ways for the international system, states that would otherwise have very little power.

Another competitive approach is unison strategies, which emphasize the role of coordination and collaboration. An organization rarely competes alone, and increasingly, the various open or contract networks rise in importance. Togetherness will make a difference here—whom to partner with may also be a competitive issue, as the most desirable partners will have a choice. Who would not want to be Google's partner today (provided that you can get a fair deal)? Its two competitors, Microsoft and Yahoo!, have formed an alliance to fight Google in online advertising. Finally, there are confrontational strategies, such as the historically ill-reputed divide-and-conquer approach that works to deny the enemy (or the suppressed people) the capability to work together so as to attack effectively.

Another such confrontational strategy is that of containment, famously defined during the U.S. cold war with the Soviet Union (1947 to 1989) by George Kennan, a career Foreign Service officer. "The main element of any United States policy toward the Soviet Union," Kennan wrote, "must be that of a long-term, patient but firm and vigilant containment of Russian expansive tendencies." To that end, he called for countering "Soviet pressure against the free institutions of the Western world" through the "adroit and vigilant application of counter-force at a series of constantly shifting geographical and political points, corresponding to the shifts and maneuvers of Soviet policy." Such a policy, Kennan predicted, would "promote tendencies which must eventually find their outlet in either the break-up or the gradual mellowing of Soviet power." (Source: www.state.gov/r/pa/ho/time/cwr/17601.htm.)

Competition may also mean the destruction of or the submission of the other party (or parties). Competitive logic, then, implies the opportunity for the use of raw force but also for cunning—beating the opponent or enemy with wit and surprise. Such strategies of brutal or witty encounter are called here "confrontational strategies" due to their nature as opportunistic and dependent on interaction and/or engagement. Surprise and mobility were Napoleon's stock–in-trade in warfare, though Liddel Hart (1968) criticizes his obsession with the idea of battle, which cost Napoleon dearly in the demoralization of French troops in Moscow in 1812. Victorious were the strategies for evasion, practiced so successfully by Kutuzov against Napoleon. Kutuzov, of course, had the advantage of being able to retreat all the way to Siberia if need be.

TYPES OF STRATEGIES

Sources of Sustained Advantage

(Non)competitive strategies	• Unique customer insight, superior industry know-how, managerial competence, operational efficiency • Rare, inimitable, or nonsubstitutable underlying resources and/or competencies • Erection and/or existence of entry barriers to potential competitors • Monopolistic market rights (for example, ownership of intellectual property) • Unique control of critical resources
Unison strategies	• Divided and/or dispersed and hence ineffective opposition • Unreproducible or unimitable complementarities in resources or competencies • Lowest partner and/or network transaction and/or coordination costs

(continued)

Confrontational or containment strategies	• Better visibility to partner and/or network activity (and hence superior capability to exploit opportunity)
	• Barriers to exiting from partnership
	• Use of raw force or cunning
	• Fear of attack or ridicule (therefore submitting or giving in)
	• Surveillance and/or alertness (that is difficult or impossible to evade)
	• Counterforce

How do the different strategies contribute to resilience? The table in the sidebar "Types of Strategies and the Links to Resilience" suggests a number of links ranging from excellence; agility [as described in *Fast Strategy* by Doz and Kosonen (2008)]; dominance in (non)competitive strategies; to presence and determination in confrontational or containment strategies. Unison strategies bring trust as their resilience strength. Trust (Fukuyama, 1995) has been shown to lower transaction costs in business and social dealings in general.

TYPES OF STRATEGIES AND THE LINKS TO RESILIENCE

(Non)competitive strategies	• *Excellence* in critical areas of business
	• *Agility* to chase opportunity with unique resources and/or competencies
	• *Dominance* to hinder competition
Unison strategies	• *Trust:* Lower negotiation costs for shifting (and covered*) strategy positions and (re)combinatorial strengths

Confrontational or containment strategies	• *Presence:* Being able to exploit an opportunity that arrives in a flash (like the martial arts) • *Determination:* Not to give in, fight every advance

* The partner "provides cover" while moving from one strategy position to another.

It is important to make a distinction between strategy and resilience here: while a strategy may be successful at a point in time (such as market dominance), resilience is a matter of long term survival (that is, it is a quality of the organization using the strategy or strategies over time). Divide and conquer, though initially successful, will likely have harmful consequences in the long term—witness the consequences of such strategies in the lands held by the British Empire such as Afghanistan. Thus resilience does not spring solely from a particular use of strategy, even if it can be tested through such strategy contests. The argument is therefore asymmetric: the test and the wellspring of resilience are separate. This partly explains why many books about excellent companies are humbled by these companies' failing to outperform in the years to come after the publication.

Therefore, resilience—in the competitive logic—is a matter of strategy *and* its consequences, which establish the advantage or disadvantage of being able to survive the long term and pursue opportunities in the long term. For instance, a strategy that brings complacency as one of its eventual or inevitable consequences will eventually fault in resilience: most empires fall. Thus strategy may contribute to resilience, but it is not its origin or cause.

The First Etiology of Resilience

Strategy + Consequences = Resilience (or Lack Thereof)

Legitimacy

The second test of resilience relies on a different survival logic: that of institutional legitimacy. Such legitimacy is a very different justification for survival than competition because it is *about* the establishment. The very word *institution* suggests staying power beyond momentary challenges. Institutions tend to perpetuate almost purely by force of their having done so in the past (they may of course still have some legitimate reasons to exist too). They have become interwoven with the people's and society's everyday life; they have *acquired* the right to exist. They offer the comfort of routine and apparent order. Institutions, as the recent banking crisis reminded us, may also survive not because of their beneficial influences on the surrounding society but because of their potential ability to wreak havoc (hence "too big to fail"). Cambridge University, for instance, encourages fierce competition among its constituent colleges, but it will not allow the weak ones to fail. The richer colleges pay to support the poorer ones; thus, Trinity College, the wealthiest, pays millions of pounds in institutional (or "university") taxes.

Therefore, according to the institutional logic, resilience is a matter of the strength of legacy (the strength of the organization's history) and its institutional depth (the degree to which the organization is embedded and interwoven into the society). Such resilience allows the institution to benefit from and depend on resources beyond its own for survival.

The Second Etiology of Resilience

Legacy + Institutional Depth = Resilience (or Lack Thereof)

The danger of this structure is that when the institutional embeddedness is very deep, should the organization fail, it may have a big impact on the surrounding society, creating "systemic" damage. The society becomes collateral to the institution's failing. Again, the recent financial crisis is a shining example of such failure—the trillion-dollar costs of which were paid by the U.S. taxpayers alone.

Sheer Toughness

The third test of resilience is one of battle hardiness. Through toughness or agility, an organization may have survived many confrontations that have tested its mettle. Toughness is, at least in part, an earned quality. Armies are tested in battles. The best companies look for competition to stay fit (and tough). Toyota, despite facing formidable U.S. competition from GM,

Ford, and Chrysler while seeking to build its business after World War II, rose to become the world's largest car manufacturer (before losing its way in 2009). Nokia rose to the world's largest mobile phone maker from near bankruptcy in the late 1980s. Similarly, Apple has been on the run after having had a difficult time in the 1990s.

According to the toughness logic, resilience is a matter of experiencing hardship, which may have led to diminished expectations and increased self-confidence for survival. It is about making do with very little (and thriving on resource scarcity). The Finns, having lived through and survived as a nation a number of wars with their much bigger Eastern neighbor, know toughness. The Winter War of 1939 to 1940, which the Finns fought against the invading Soviets, is an example of tenacity against all odds. *Sisu*, the Finnish word for tenacity, means not giving up—no matter what. (It is often said that Finns know how to deal with hardship but are rather baffled by success, which they suspect poses a subtle threat to the ability to stay clear-minded.) Hardship develops character, they say.

The Third Etiology of Resilience

Experience of Hardship + (Diminished Expectations
  ÷ Increased Determination) = Resilience (or Lack Thereof)

The "Summary of the Logics That Contribute to Resilience" sidebar shows the characteristics of the competitive, institutional, and survival logics.

SUMMARY OF THE LOGICS THAT CONTRIBUTE TO RESILIENCE

Competitive Logics
  Value creation
  Collaboration
  Dominance

Institutional Logics
  Heritage or promise: Stand for something.
  Legitimacy
  Ability to wreak havoc (too big to fail)

(continued)

Survival Logics
Battle hardy
Strong core (identity)
Resource-scarce survival

PERFORMANCE ASSESSMENT

It is imperative to assess corporate performance from three perspectives: strategy relevance, operational efficiency, and corporate resilience. *Strategy relevance* is about engaging the people with whom you wish to do business. *Operational efficiency* is about the productivity and resource consumption of such a pursuit. *Corporate resilience* is about the capacity to survive the short term while being able to accomplish strategic transformation in the long term (that is, turn threats into opportunities).

THREE CRITICAL PERSPECTIVES ON CORPORATE PERFORMANCE

1. *Strategy relevance:* How engaging are you to the people with whom you wish to do business?
2. *Operational efficiency:* How productive are you? How efficient is the effort in terms of resources consumed?
3. *Corporate resilience:* How often are you able to turn threats into opportunities before they have become clearly visible?

HUMAN FALLIBILITY AND THE SAMPLE OF ONE

Sadly, the overall human record of resilient action is poor. To quote Fukuyama (2007: 172):

> We can predict with certainty that we will be surprised; we can and do anticipate an array of catastrophic events. Unfortunately, [. . .] we can also predict with certainty that when they come, we will be inadequately prepared.

Part of the reason for this dark prediction is that the absence of a surprise or a catastrophe (which might indicate luck or good resilience) tends to increase temptation for discounting the probability of an event like that happening, and hence reducing (costly) preparation measures. Thus the better job we do in resilience, the less we are willing to invest in it (paradoxically, something that is working marvelously).

It is difficult in our minds to differentiate between the frequency of an event and its probability: something not having happened in the past makes us trust that it won't happen in the future either. We should *not* trust this probability calculator of ours. Our past experience (of event frequency) is a poor guide for future probabilities.

As listed in the sidebar "Interpreting Experience," a number of reasons complicate resilient action, due to human cognition.

INTERPRETING EXPERIENCE

The Nature of Human Cognition

1. Time frames of interests ("In the long term, we are all dead.")
2. Biases and heuristics (Decision-making habits and anchors, the surprise of rare events.)
3. Confusion between frequencies and probabilities (Direct experience is a poor guide.)
4. Narrative fallacies (A good story beats the facts.)
5. Beliefs in corroborative evidence and/or the problem of induction (We find what we are looking for.)

One reason that taking resilient action is difficult is because we are not very good at interpreting experience. Another reason is that we induce that if something has never happened before in our experience, it is sufficient proof that it will not happen in the future[1] [also known as "the problem of corroborative evidence" (see Taleb, 2007: All swans we have seen are white. Therefore, there are no black swans)]. However, just one observation that disproves a state of affairs is sufficient for a stronger conclusion. (Popperian falsification: There is one black swan; therefore, not all swans are white). Humans in general are not very good at making evidence-based conclusions. But let us take some blame off: Our experience is admittedly rather thin—after all, we have only our own lives, consisting of a few decades, to draw inferences from. How do you generalize from a case study (our own)? Thus, we, living our sample of one, lack a reasonable basis for making judgments.

B. H. Liddel Hart (1968), a famous proponent of the indirect approach as a military strategy, has written the following:

> Direct experience is inherently too limited to form an adequate foundation either for theory or for application. At the best it produces an atmosphere that is of value in drying and hardening the structure of thought. The greatest value in indirect experience lies in its greater variety and extent. (pp. 23–24)

Therefore, the essence of being resilient is learning without experience. Professor Risto Tainio at the Helsinki School of Economics talks about the hard way of learning: making the mistake oneself and learning from the failure as opposed to the easy way of learning—learning from someone else's experience without having to experience (the failure) oneself. Or, as Bismarck is quoted as having said: "Fools say they learn by experience. I prefer to profit by others' experience." This capacity to learn from others can be extended to learning from near events, requisite imagination, and analogues. We have the capacity to consider the most extreme case—what the situation might be like taken to its logical limit or conclusion. This kind of mental gymnastics adds potentially significantly to resilience and lowers the cost of learning, by eliminating a potentially disastrous failure.

For example, March, Sproull, and Tamuz (1991: 11) suggest a number of strategies to "learn from samples of one or fewer." Among them is the notion that one should "experience history richly," which involves paying attention to different experiences as part of a decision. For example, one must not only consider the decision's consequences but also the "collateral consequences associated with the making of the decision and its implementation" (p. 2). History can also be experienced more richly by experiencing multiple interpretations of what happened, such as the telling of stories from multiple stakeholder perspectives and experiencing more preferences by changing aspiration levels such as definitions for success. History can further be simulated by considering "near histories," such as accidents that *almost* happened or other hypothetical histories, including future scenarios. Such strategies may help improve the handicap we have in making sense of the limited experience we have.

FOUR QUESTIONS IN MAKING USE OF ENRICHED EXPERIENCE

1. What is the evidential standing of imagination?
2. What is the proper process for combining prior expectations and interrelated, cumulative aspects of a rich description into an interpretation of history?
3. What is the proper trade-off between reliability and validity in historical interpretation?
4. What are the relative values of multiple observations of events and multiple interpretations of them?

Source: March, Sproull, and Tamuz (1991: 11).

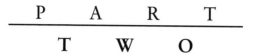

STEP 1.
MANAGING THE
CONSEQUENCES
OF PAST
PERFORMANCE

No CEO starts with a clean slate. It is tempting to think about how to achieve great performance and, in the process, ignore the legacy of past performance. However, this legacy may strongly resist change, depriving the organization of resilience. Hence managing the consequences of past performance is the first step toward building a more resilient organization.

In the recent, industry-shaping debate, President Barack Obama said that if the United States were starting from a clean slate, a "single-payer" health-care system would be preferable to the other systems proposed. "If I were starting a system from scratch, then I think that the idea of moving toward a single-payer system could very well make sense," Obama said, according to National Public Radio, June 22, 2009. "The only problem is that we're not starting from scratch." Indeed, the U.S. health-care system is trapped in a web of powerful economic interests. Such a radical shift from the existing employer-paid insurance system to a government-paid insurance system would be arguably too disruptive for the current $2.2 trillion health-care industry.

Similarly, a much smaller change effort, the cash-for-clunkers program, included a clause that cars built before 1984 (the *real* clunkers) were not eligible. Why? Because of the interests of the automobile lobbies, which include car collectors and parts resellers.

Thus reasonable programs with laudable aims are reshaped by vested interests, and there is no clean break from the past because "you cannot change an entire health-care industry in one legislation" or there are lobbyists that those successful in the past can afford to employ. (The automobile aftermarket business is huge.) Future success, on the other hand, has few lobby groups. Who would pay for it? Hopefully our elected representatives will stand for the possibility of success in the future for those not yet institutionalized as parties of note. It is the American dream too!

PERFORMANCE TRAPS

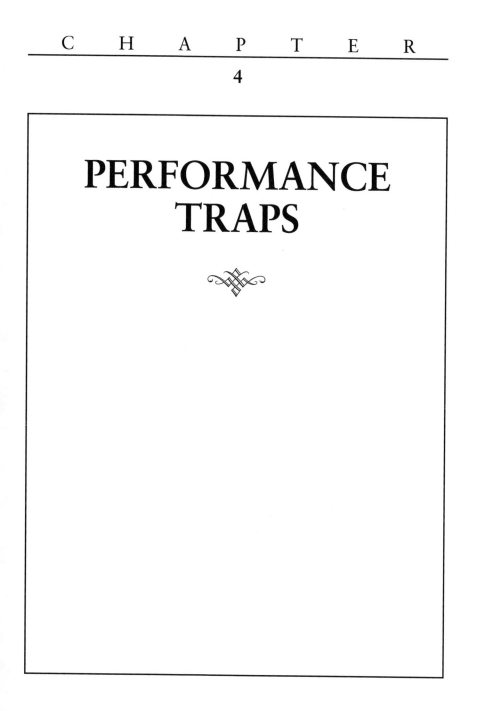

It is all well and good to try and seek great performance in the future by managing from the future back, but unless the potentially toxic consequences of past performance are tamed, no resilience can be achieved (see the sidebar "Summary of the Toxic Consequences of Past Performance"). Why? Because high success in the past has, over and over again, been seen to result in effects that are known to be detrimental to continued success. Examples of these effects are overconfidence, hubris, and undue attribution of merit to oneself (the fallacy of "I deserved it," which has been shown to emerge even in clinical tests where the "winner" is assigned randomly). Kets de Vries, in *Leaders, Fools, and Impostors* (2003), recounts multiple stories in which, eventually, the exercise of executive power leads to outrageous, risky, pathological, bad judgment–encroached acts. Why did then CEO of Enron, Jeffrey Skilling, call attendees in an earnings call "idiots" (a short time before Enron fell)? It was hubris talking. Tellingly, the 2003 *Fortune* editors' documentary about Enron is titled *The Smartest Guys in the Room*.

Similarly, the London-headquartered bank HSBC acquired the consumer finance firm Household International for $14.2 billion and "surprised Wall Street" at the height of its drive to expand to the United States. Having run into severe difficulty due to subprime mortgage losses, multiple sources claim the bank later admitted that "with the benefit of hindsight, this is an acquisition we wish we had not undertaken; . . . the takeover was an absolute disaster." Yet it was at its conclusion hailed as the "deal of the first decade of the twenty-first century" by a U.K. banking journal (*Banker*, October 6, 2003). The lesson is: When you are at the very height of the performance curve, it is *really* time to be careful.

But past performance management should not be limited to extreme success only—mediocre and poor performances are equally dangerous. Think of past performance, no matter how good or bad, as the enemy of resilience because therein lies many of the company's vulnerabilities.

SUMMARY OF THE TOXIC CONSEQUENCES OF PAST PERFORMANCE

High Success
- Overconfidence (or insecurity compensation)
- Hubris in one's competence
- Undue attribution of merit to self
- Structural hardening, rigidity
- Immoderation and escalation of success formula
- Lost capacity for experimentation
- Attentive complacency

Mediocre Performance
- Conventional thinking
- Best people leaving
- Lowered aspirations
- Similarly unambitious reference groups
- Interests groups forming to perpetuate status quo
- Control of resources by those who benefit from mediocrity

Very Low Performance
- Failure traps
- Threat-rigidity response
- Extreme risk taking in case survival is threatened
- Inward-focused attention
- No one cares. Everyone has given up.

WHY GOOD COMPANIES GO BAD

- Strategic frames create blinders.
- Processes cause routines.
- Relationships become shackles.
- Values become dogmas. (Sull, 1999: 45)

The very characteristics that made a company highly successful now work against it, making it unable to adapt to new market demands precisely because those existing characteristics were the reason for prior success (and thus they are heavily entrenched and honored as ways of working). Not because they do not do anything. But because they keep doing the wrong things. This is what Sull calls "active inertia." For example, it is currently difficult for Dell, the online computer seller, to change its ways to compete with Hewlett-Packard, which has a more diverse customer engagement model (and sells a lot of printer ink too).

Other researchers already noted the paradox earlier: "An example of processes of inertia is Miller's research (1993; Miller & Chen, 1994) demonstrating that inertia is often the unintended consequence of successful performance. Successful organizations discard practices, people, and structures regarded as peripheral to success and grow more inattentive to signals that suggest the need for change, more insular and sluggish in adaptation, and more immoderate in their processes, tending toward extremes of risk-taking or conservatism. These changes simplify the organization, sacrifice adaptability, and increase inertia" (Weick & Quinn, 1999: 369). Further, D'Aveni found an enemy of resilience in that "pure profit maximizing behavior may be at the expense of organizational survival" (D'Aveni & MacMillan, 1990: 135).

SUCCESS IS A GREAT SLAVE BUT A POOR HOST

Malcolm Gladwell, in his book *Outliers* (2008), suggests that the story of success is essentially a matter of luck, whereas Jim Collins, in his book *How the Mighty Fall* (2009: 119), claims that there are "principles of greatness" companies can practice. Whom do you believe? Both are probably right—once you get lucky, practicing greatness is well advised. Surely you can even increase the odds of becoming great (somewhat) by your own actions (as captured in Collins's previous book *Good to Great*). However, relying on very generic recommendations such as "choose the right people to lead" can be hazardous. What if you make a mistake? Weick and Sutcliffe (2007: 70–71) talk about FedEx Global Operations Control's achievement of moving 100 percent of the packages on time as an example of resilience "despite the presence of adversity . . . such as . . . lousy leadership and performance, and production pressures."

I believe the outlier condition—that is, high success—is not something easily repeated with a formula that once worked well. For example, once Microsoft became dominant in PC software, it was decidedly more difficult for other software companies to do the same, as the market players had learned their surprise lesson. An entirely new "business model," open source software—with its very different style of voluntary organizing, problem-solving motives, and peer values—had instead gained dominance.

This is not to say that success does not include organizational characteristics that can be generalized. It is simply to point out that most of these exalted but idiosyncratic characteristics are already known; they're just very hard to replicate on the strength of that knowledge. In other words, knowing the principles of greatness is not very likely to make you great (beyond hard work and luck, perhaps the only two enduring lessons of the past). You will have to discover your own. As the Finnish songwriter Juice Leskinen once sang: "It is the misfortune of followers to make dogma out of the wisdom of their leaders." (Religious and other extremists, take note!)

Some of these generic wisdoms are full of contradiction. Arrogance, for example, is well known as an enemy to continued success, and thus it is a rather bad host if it gains the upper hand in a person or organization. Yet arrogance often also connotes the unfettered ambition and uncompromising spirit needed for extraordinary success. This kind of demanding attitude may actually describe successful entrepreneurs such as Apple's Steve Jobs, who is known for his perfectionist nature (as defined by his standards of "insanely great" products). Intel's Andy Grove was known for his impatience with getting results (or answers to his questions). In my own experience, you have about five minutes to come up with a relevant argument when talking to most CEOs—after that, you're out.

If you manage to resolve the dilemma that a group of researchers from AT&T's famed Bell Labs once called "humbition"—being humble but having great ambition at the same time—there are a number of good enough, if mundane, ideas for improvement out there. ("Eat your own dog food" was the Silicon Valley mantra for using the company's own products and services to make sure to know what they are like and thus putting oneself in the customer's position.) The problem is that the humbleness tends to wear out quickly and give way to complacency. Success, then, comes with the almost irresistible feeling of entitlement, formula-perpetuating routines, and established power coalitions (see the "Dangers and Seductions of Success" sidebar). It is also tempting to think that everyone else is out there to serve you and your interests (yet it is difficult to get a truly independent assessment from those potentially sharing the success).

VOICE OF RESILIENCE

One of my colleagues and I once met with a renowned management consultant. After the meeting, which was allegedly intended to explore opportunities for collaboration, my colleague said, "I have never before in my life felt so much like an instrument to someone else's purposes." This colleague was an unusually resilient one (and has since made a fantastic career for himself).

Most people lose their ability to think independently when face-to-face with high success, to the point that it dims their capacity for smart action. They agree to things they would not otherwise consider, for instance. Partly this may be blamed on a deep human tendency for imitation, and when the object is illustrious success, we wish to imitate it even more. Moreover, highly successful people also suffer from not being able to trust what people say to them—not because their supporters intentionally lie but because success tends to distort reality in an attempt to replicate itself in the future. If you are extremely successful, most people agree with you, no matter what you say; or at least they will not readily criticize. Often they are seeking a piece of your success. If they do not kill you ("E tu, Brute!"), they will be subservient to you. Their opinions are colored by your opinions and thus not reliable. This is a bad recipe for the continuation of success. You must take drastic action so that your past success does not entirely cloud the attitude and advice of people around you.

Kleiner (2003: 75) has written: "When you are a Core Group member, your remarks are automatically amplified. . . . Casually mention a product you'd like to develop someday, and you'll discover three weeks later that someone has spent a million dollars introducing it. . . . Why does this happen? Because nobody knows exactly what you want. They assume it is part of their job to guess. They may be too intimidated by your Core Group status and the legitimacy you've acquired in their minds to ask."

DANGERS AND SEDUCTIONS OF SUCCESS

Mental or Cognitive

1. Hubris (ungrounded and unrealistic can-do attitude)
2. Narcissism (an excessive hunger for power and fame for their own sake, Kets de Vries, 2003)
3. Arrogance (not listening to others, not being open to others' opinions)
4. Feeling of entitlement (of being uniquely deserving without corresponding cause or merit)
5. Complacency (the numbing of senses, the lack of motivation to continue to excel or prove oneself)
6. Inattention (paying less and less attention to issues that do not fit the current operations and/or strategy or agenda)

Behavioral

1. Overdoing what one does best (exploitation); neglecting what one could do eventually well (exploration)
2. Scaling up a once successful formula to its absurdity (or to the point where entirely new, perhaps systemic, risks are created)
3. Being solely focused on an activity that is losing market relevance or is about to be "disrupted" (technologically or through a different business model)
4. Replicating success to the point where all diversity of the system disappears (for example, hiring people who all have exactly the same educational background or mindset)

Political

1. Power coalitions and dependencies (for example, entrenched and vested interests)
2. No free resources (all existing resources already committed and invested in existing businesses with in-company leadership)
3. No perceivably better business opportunities (at least in the short term; all alternative opportunities yield less than the current businesses); lack of political will to invest
4. The target to beat (competitors unite against the dominant one)
5. The one to blame ("Public Enemy Number 1")

While it is difficult, perhaps occasionally impossible, to avoid the dangers of success, all enslavements do suggest ways toward an escape. These are good remedies, but they are not likely in themselves to create a resilient organization. Managing past success is but a good first step.

MEDIOCRITY IS HARD TO BEAT

A Japanese Nobel Prize winner once exclaimed, "We are continuously contaminated by conventional thinking." This is the temptation and hazard of mediocrity—hard-to-escape daily orthodoxy, or a pervasive lack of imagination and aspiration. This dulling fog lowers performance as our aspirations level off, and we become satisfied with our performance relative to others with a vested interest in not challenging the status quo. (Conversely, should you wish to improve, choose another, radically better reference group!)

In most companies, by this stage, the imaginative and brave people have already left. Note that a defining sign of mediocrity is its conventionality—eschewing risk taking and shying away from new ideas (March, 1991). Here is a test: How many innovators are left in your company from the last high-profile innovation consulting project? There is little hope for continued strength of performance unless the company can keep its best people and ideas from leaving.

Here is the path to the dulling of the senses:

1. Great people leave (usually in frustration).
2. Orthodoxy settles in and grows. Aspirations are lowered. Reference groups form that do not challenge the orthodoxy.
3. A core group (one or more) forms to perpetuate its ability to benefit from the organization.
4. Risks are avoided that would jeopardize the core group's stranglehold (see Kleiner, 2003). There are few if any incentives to search for higher performance.
5. Resources are not allocated based on performance but based on the (now powerful) core group's control of the organization (for example, Pfeffer & Salancik, 1978).

6. The organization has become "permanently failing" with stakeholders keeping the performance at the level they can benefit from (Meyer & Zucker, 1989).
7. The core group gains legitimacy and therefore will be hard to unseat on performance grounds alone.

So, to beat mediocrity, the core group has to be unseated. Otherwise, it has no incentive to stop milking the organizational cow. To do that, you will not only have to challenge its performance but demerit its legitimacy. This amounts to a coup d'état, a political revolution. Good luck! You'll need it! (For examples of how to go about such a revolution, see Chapter 10, "Case Study: Imaginative Thinking in Action—The Case of the ODDsters," and Chapter 13, "Postcard No. 3 from San Jose, California: Tempered Radicalism and Management Practices That Stick.")

VERY LOW PERFORMANCE INVITES CALAMITY

While it is possible to perpetuate mediocrity, very low performance has its destabilizing characteristics.

Very low performance results in the diverging of the core group's interests, as the organization can no longer sustain all of its elite. In the event of a major adversity that threatens the organization, the organization falls back on its old routines, which may be inappropriate (or even what got the company in present trouble in the first place). It is easy to fall into a failure trap (Levinthal & March, 1993) because even if a particular strategy might eventually work, there is either no patience for it, or time simply runs out before giving the strategy a chance to show its might. There is no time for experimental learning or for developing a portfolio of strategic options. Usually huge risks need to be taken so that the organization has at least a chance of survival (which requires radical, yet untested and unrehearsed change). Turnaround is attempted, at huge human and financial costs. A corporate turnaround specialist is called in. Attention tends to become focused inward, thus further isolating the organization from changes in its competitive environment.

The company may have to purchase its momentary survival at the expense of future viability.

FEATURES OF VERY LOW PERFORMANCE

- Threat-rigidity syndrome (paralyzed to inaction in the face of a threat)
- Failure trap (changing direction too often, without giving any strategy a chance to work)
- High risk taking (seeing drastic action as the only chance for survival)
- Inward-focused attention (internal fighting, blame games)
- High cost of change (no time for experimental learning or option development)

Since most of us, like President Obama upon entering the White House, cannot start from "a clean slate," we should carefully manage the potential of past performance to be the enemy of resilience. High success has its well-known dangers in excess, mediocrity needs something to shake itself off, and very low performance tends to run out of road. The sidebar "Tip Book on Overcoming Past Performance: Breaking Out" summarizes this chapter, but it is presented here first and foremost as an inspiration for you to start thinking about this difficult issue.

TIP BOOK ON OVERCOMING PAST PERFORMANCE: BREAKING OUT

1. Find ways to experience situations that are truly novel to you. (How are they challenging you?)
2. Give up all the luxury and rights of comfort for a week. Try out a life without entitlements. (Live a week on a student budget.)
3. Go find the best team in the world in your area of specialization, and work with this team for a while. (How do you feel?)
4. Start 10 small experiments and run them for one to three months to attack an ill-defined or persisting problem. (What did you learn?)

(continued)

5. Spend some time with people whose worldviews are radically different from yours. (What did you talk about together? Which experiences have been formative in their worldviews?)
6. Read about 10 primary ideas out there, and think about them. (Which ideas best represent you and your behavior?)
7. Start a company dedicated to social entrepreneurship, and try to hire people to run it. (Why did they agree to join?)
8. Try to live a week in a way that is truly sustainable, leaving no irrecoverable footprint. (What did you give up?)

CASE STUDY: INNOVATION TRAUMA AND RESILIENCE

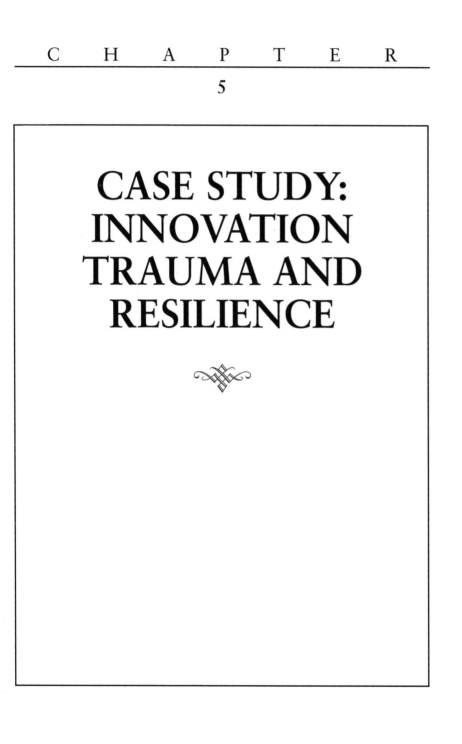

A very important part of performance management is to avoid the trauma that high-risk or high-passion endeavors, such as innovation, are prone to. Here is a story that encompasses trauma from innovation (linked to thin-computing client called the Sun Ray at Sun Microsystems,[1] once a very promising computing innovation) and some thoughts toward how such debilitative side effects can be avoided. Innovation is an important aspect of performance—often acclaimed as *the* source of competitive advantage—yet it has a dark side rarely talked about. This dark side is critical to acknowledge in any performance management discussion since only a very few succeed as initially hoped and most actually fail. This failure tends to be highly emotional and carry huge organizational consequences, and it is potentially a major enemy of resilience if left unattended.

This discussion is based on an article I coauthored with Martin Hoegl and Michael Gibbert titled, "Why Learning from Failure Isn't Easy (and What to Do about It): Innovation Trauma at Sun Microsystems."[2] The original case study was written with Jay Moldenhauer-Salazar who at the time was the director of Sun's Human Resources Labs.

CAUSES OF INNOVATION TRAUMA

Common wisdom suggests that "you learn more from your failures than your successes." However, I find this is not always true for failed innovations in organizations. In fact, there are instances when one failed innovation in an otherwise successful organization "traumatizes" the team and weakens its spirit permanently. The ill effects of such trauma include not only missed lessons from the failure but also the possibility of causing a new failure (precisely because of missed learnings from the earlier failure).

As with any organizational success or failure, there are likely several key reasons for the performance of the Sun Ray, the computing innovation in question. The case description hints to some exogenous (for example, at the time Microsoft's and Intel's dominance of the PC industry was growing fast) and endogenous (for example, strategic positioning, project overstaffing) factors. In this case, however, the spotlight is on innovation trauma as one critical driver of failure. And in this situation, as is usually true in most organizations, there were early warning signals of the trauma as well as possible treatments, so that learning from inevitable failures could empower innovators to embark on the next project with confidence.

The case of the Sun Ray is an example of a situation in which a prior innovation failure—that of JavaStation—caused innovation trauma. I, together with my colleagues Professor Michael Gibbert, Bocconi University, and Martin Hoegl, WHU Otto Beisheim School of Management, in the related study, propose this trauma had traveled to Sun Ray, a conceptually similar but technologically superior product. The emotional costs experienced by the Sun Ray engineering team and the marketing department ultimately deprived the Sun Ray of a fair trial as a radical innovation. This posttraumatic disorder even affected some members of upper management, who had been burned by the JavaStation experience.

Our study of the Sun Ray leads us then to suggest that managers should pay more attention to moderating the contagious trauma that innovators may experience. Given the oscillating nature of innovation in the form of internal venturing activities (Burgelman & Välikangas, 2005), coping with failure becomes particularly important. But paradoxically, learning from failure is difficult under conditions of innovation trauma, as the Sun Ray case illustrates.

Management practices may mediate the emotional cost of failure and begin to build the conditions for learning from failure. Management practices for healing, in case the trauma has already occurred, should be developed in order to offer relief and/or help people to move on without shying away from innovation activity in the future. Innovators should be allowed to learn from their past experiences to hone their skills as advanced innovators, rather than becoming "innovation gun-shy." This study thus addresses a challenge familiar to most managers of innovative processes in organizations: having to reject many more ideas and initiatives than one is able to accept, while keeping the innovators' enthusiasm and emotional engagement (a most critical ingredient for success) alive. It is worth investing in innovators to prevent them from becoming cynics or dropouts—the default paths for traumatized innovators.

WHY LEARNING FROM FAILURE ISN'T EASY (AND WHAT TO DO ABOUT IT)

Innovations fail at an alarming rate. Depending on the product category, estimates range from between 40 and 90 percent (Gourville, 2006). Explanations for failure are manifold and include product-based, developer-based, and consumer-based reasons for failure (for example, Rogers, 1995; Moore, 1991).

But by far the most common explanation hinges on the individuals carrying the innovation forward. Researchers have argued that such factors as wishful thinking, overconfidence or even arrogance, escalation of commitment, or plain ignorance are to blame. The common denominator among these views is that emotional or ego involvement stands in the way of innovation. For example, developers may "fall in love with the technology and forget the markets it needs to serve" (Schnarrs, 1988).

We argue that not only can ego involvement stand in the way of innovation but it can also damage confidence: innovators become gun-shy after a failed innovation. We refer to this as *innovation trauma*. And while the ideal of learning from failure is a good one, empirical research on innovation projects indicates no systematic relationship between the degree of project success (or failure) and the amount of learning team members report stemming from the same project (Hoegl & Gemuenden, 2001). It seems entirely intuitive, though, to assume that lessons from previous mistakes help future undertakings. So why doesn't it always hold true? The reason is that innovative tasks naturally carry high risks (technical and market risks), and their success often hinges on the unwavering commitment of various individuals involved. Team members and management sponsors need to be personally and emotionally engaged to drive key innovations forward. If and when such innovations fail, we have to expect significant posttraumatic disorders lingering for some time and getting in the way of learning from future projects.

Individual trauma is defined by psychologists as an extreme condition "outside the usual human experience, ... a serious threat to his or her life or physical integrity" (Kahn, 2003: 365). In organizational literature, trauma is seen as a possible by-product of change (such as layoffs) that has a high personal cost to individual employees (D'Aveni & MacMillan, 1990; Iacovini, 1993; Weick, 1988). A crisis that necessitates severe measures for which the organization (and consequently, its employees) is not prepared, may cause trauma (Amabile & Conti, 1999; also Hamel & Välikangas, 2003). We define *innovation trauma* as the inability to commit to a new innovation due to severe disappointment from previous innovation failures (for example, new products rejected by the market or the company's top management). As such, rather than learning from failure and utilizing such new knowledge in subsequent projects, innovation trauma inhibits the personal and emotional investment necessary to achieve high innovation performance henceforth.

Thus, let us ask: What does it take to learn more from our failures, rather than letting them drag down subsequent innovation endeavors? Putting the spotlight on the traumatic experience itself, we first show how innovation trauma played out as Sun Microsystems tried to launch a thin-computing client technology called the Sun Ray in the aftermath of the miserably unsuccessful JavaStation. This case serves as an illustration identifying critical antecedents and symptoms of innovation trauma. We then turn to key moderators that can minimize the detrimental effects of innovation trauma on an organization's innovative capabilities: How can innovation trauma be treated so as to enable organizations to learn from inevitable failures?

INNOVATION TRAUMA AT SUN MICROSYSTEMS

As is often the case with innovation, the story begins with a dream and lots of hard work (see "About This Case Study" at the end of this chapter for a description of our two-year research project). The Sun Ray was intended to change an industry. The "simple, low-cost device, which requires no desktop administration," was launched at the Enterprise Computing Forum in New York City in September 1999 at a price of $399 per unit. It was considered a revolution in desktop computing: The Sun Ray redefined what "desktop computing" meant.[3] If you worked on a Sun Ray, you could hop from terminal to terminal—around the world—picking up where you last left off in a matter of seconds because your desktop was virtually and instantly created through the network connection. New software upgrades would appear automatically each time you logged in. If someone stole your Sun Ray, he or she would get a hunk of metal and plastic with exactly zero proprietary information in it.

The Sun Ray exhibited some other benefits too. When Sun Microsystems switched from Sun workstations to Sun Rays in 2000, the company saved more than $2 million in electricity costs alone because the Sun Ray demanded so little power to run. Its sleek design was impressive too, and the product appealed to many. A number of executives have told us the Sun Ray had perhaps the best demo of a product they had ever seen. Otherwise critical journalists liked it too: for example, read the glowing review of the demo by Rich Karlgaard in *Forbes*, January 2003.[4]

Still, despite the high hopes, the Sun Ray never sold anywhere near the 100,000 units Sun had expected in the first year, much less the 1 million Sun forecasted for year 2. Throughout its first six years of existence, the Sun Ray struggled to land even one significant reference customer to tout its magnificence. In fact, if you don't work in the high-tech industry, you have probably never even heard of the Sun Ray. In many ways, you can add it to the pile of other novel computing ideas (like Apple Computer's Newton) as yet another radical innovation that failed to generate significant wealth for its creators.

When it comes to *radical innovation*, we follow the definition put forward by Dewar and Dutton (1986: 1422–1423): "Radical innovations ... represent revolutionary changes in technology" as well as ideas, practices, or material artifacts that are "perceived to be new by the relevant unit of adoption" and "represent clear departures from existing practice." The Sun Ray represented a marked departure from Microsoft-dominated personal-computing technology at a time when it perhaps was not too late to introduce competing technology infrastructures to rival PCs. Furthermore, its target customers were not individuals but organizations such as call centers or health-care providers that required cheap, reliable computing power. The Sun Ray was much less costly to manage as a computing solution than a

PC, and it offered protection against data theft. Today, its green credentials in saving electricity would be even more appreciated.

Although the Sun Ray's failure to generate significant wealth is a common new technology story, we think the reasons behind this failure point to an often-neglected but important culprit. The Sun Ray failed, in part, as a product launch because its predecessor, the much-hyped JavaStation (Sun's hoped-for Microsoft killer), had been an engineering disaster. It was JavaStation's prior failure (discussed in the following section) that crippled the Sun Ray internally at Sun Microsystems, independent of the Sun Ray's own potential in the marketplace, and it was Sun's inability to recover from the trauma of JavaStation's failure that prevented it from marketing the Sun Ray effectively, thus leaving open questions about its ultimate viability in the marketplace.

Before we can explore how the Sun Ray's emergent story led us into the concept of innovation trauma, it is important to first understand this case. The next section provides a brief synopsis of the effects of JavaStation's legacy on the Sun Ray over an eight-year period. Beyond the difficulty of gaining acceptance for new technologies in the marketplace, which has been addressed by many authors in innovation literature (for example, Christensen, 1997; Moore, 1991), we wish to draw attention to the reasons why learning from failed innovation doesn't come easily, and, in particular, how prior innovation failures may get in the way of effectively organizing behind a new, related innovation (see Huy, 1999). Thus our explanation is not external—that is, a matter of user adoption—but internal—that is, an issue of emotional comfort and trust with the new innovation (see Massey, 2002, about the need to integrate emotional components in social analysis).

THE EMERGENCE OF POSTTRAUMATIC DISORDERS

Development of the Sun Ray was begun in 1997 within Sun Labs, Sun's R&D laboratories, by six engineers primarily interested in multimedia technologies. These were experienced, talented engineers with complementary skills who had worked together on several projects before beginning work on what would become the Sun Ray.

Although the initial idea behind the Sun Ray can be traced to several origins, at least one spark was the existence of the JavaStation, a similar "thin-client" product that Sun marketed aggressively. As one engineer explained, "At the time that JavaStations came on the scene, we were actually looking at all the reasons why it was not going to be a success. In our minds, JavaStation was quite simply a bad idea poorly implemented." Partly as a reaction to the JavaStations, then, these engineers began tinkering with their own thin-client approach. At first each member worked only part-time on Sun Ray (then codenamed NeWT, for "network terminal"); yet the project captured their collective imagination, and soon they dropped all other work in order to focus on the Sun Ray full time.

The team debuted a Sun Ray prototype at Sun's annual Spring Leadership Conference, where Sun Labs traditionally unveiled new technologies. This internal showcase impressed numerous Sun leaders, including Scott McNealy, Sun's president and (then) CEO. Emboldened by their success, the team members looked to find a home for the Sun Ray within one of Sun's mainstream product groups. Eventually, the Sun Ray group moved into a hardware division, ironically housed in the same business unit and building as the JavaStation product.

The Sun Ray's core team grew organically and worked tirelessly. Since most of Sun's organizational attention was focused on the JavaStation, the Sun Ray group was able to operate in relative isolation. Team members reported the experience as a "start-up within Sun," an experience that provided both focus and camaraderie. Team members worked 12 to 15 hours a day, seven days a week and through holidays, not missing a single day because of illness, injury, or vacation. Their efforts paid off too, as the team went from producing a prototype followed by a final product in nine months, a Sun record at the time.

After nearly three years of investment and high expectations, the floundering JavaStation product was canceled a month before the Sun Ray's official release in 1999. As an alternative to laying off the entire group, Sun's leadership decided to combine the JavaStation team of over 200 people and the Sun Ray team of 20 people. The Sun Ray group suddenly inherited a legion of people and skills it didn't need. As one engineer recalled, "We were in a situation in which we had this huge group building stuff because we had people and not because there was a demand for it." The Sun Ray group also inherited a group whose morale was at its nadir, and the once start-up enthusiasm within the team vanished into infighting and empire building.

Thus began a series of dizzying changes for the Sun Ray. Months after the product's launch, a new leader took over the group. Over the next five years, the Sun Ray group would have six executive sponsors and four vice presidents in charge of the product. Turnover in the Sun Ray group skyrocketed, particularly in marketing, because it was perceived as an "engineering-led" team.

As the dot-com bubble burst in 2001, Sun began to experience its first downsizing in company history. Through a series of companywide layoffs, the Sun Ray group, which had grown to be a grossly inefficient 250-person group, was whittled down to be a mere 22-person group. Only Sun's internal IT group saved the product from being canceled completely, which it was able to do because the Sun Ray had become the de facto desktop with Sun employees over the course of its three-year history.

Eventually, a shell of its former self and with only one of the original engineers remaining, the Sun Ray group moved to Sun's software division. There it finally found the supporting products to enable its bundling as a desktop to customers. Java Enterprise System, complete with the Sun Ray technology, debuted in 2003, and it sparked a new wave of optimism for the Sun Ray both internally and with customers. Sun Ray sales continue today, though nowhere near their initial, optimistic projections.

Sadly for the Sun Ray, the JavaStation prevented it from gaining a fair playing field.

MISSED EARLY WARNING SIGNALS FOR INNOVATION TRAUMA WITH THE SUN RAY

This case study suggests that attention should be paid to the conditions under which innovation is likely to cause trauma. The Sun Ray example points to three early warning signals that were missed.

Trauma Breeds Cynicism

The Silicon Valley, where Sun Microsystems was founded and still has its headquarters, has been credited for its friendliness to "fail-often" culture; yet there are indications that such entrepreneurial failures are nevertheless traumatic despite their seductive (prefailure) "upside" potential. Indeed, the connotations of Schumpeter's famous term "creative destruction" are suggestive of high emotional (and other) costs.

The personal experience that an innovator feels when an innovation in which she or he (often together with a team of colleagues) has invested a substantial amount of effort and passion woefully betrays its hard-won expectations can be described as a personal and emotional loss. Furthermore, it is occasionally a frustration for future innovation pursuits, and it potentially leads to cynicism about whether innovation will ever work in the company. Interestingly, as the Sun Ray case suggests, major parts of the organization can experience innovation trauma together (the sales department, for example, as suggested earlier). Here are some telling quotes:

> *Engineering:* "The original 10 [engineers] were excited about the [Sun Ray] product release. The other 80 had just been given some choices, told 'you can work with us or work somewhere else.' . . . I think a lot of people were disgruntled that the JavaStation was killed in favor of the Sun Ray."
>
> *Sales:* "We felt we would eventually cut the product, like we did the JavaStation. The field did not trust the Sun Ray at all. A lot of field reps were burned by all the flux with JavaStation."
>
> *Customers:* "I would sit in sales calls talking about how innovative we were, and the customer would [remind us of the JavaStation] and say, 'You guys can't focus on anything!'"
>
> *Leaders:* "[An executive at Sun] was not a fan of the Sun Ray. He never got over the failure of the JavaStation."

Trauma Causes Disillusionment

The JavaStation team had just experienced the severe failure of a signature product that was heavily marketed and identified with the company to the point where it had become synonymous with the company's success. JavaStations were largely touted as the network computer that Scott McNealy and Larry Ellison claimed would dethrone Microsoft. The JavaStation team had thus been embarrassed as an engineering team not able to deliver on this promise. Said one director about his faith in the

JavaStation: "Until the JavaStation, I had thought engineering was as reliable as rain, but now I was skeptical." This unexpected "engineering" failure then caused the sales organization promoting the JavaStation to lose credibility with its clients: "A lot of field reps were burned by all the flux with the JavaStation. The joke in our group was 'Yeah, I know we said we would have the product, but we lied.'" When the salespeople were expected to try to sell the Sun Ray, they felt they could no longer trust engineering: why would the Sun Ray, which they associated with the JavaStation, work any better? The technological differences were ignored as emotions of broken trust and feelings of their own reduced credibility among clients came to the surface. Indeed, this traumatic experience may likely have interfered with the crafting of a solid marketing and sales strategy, one of the Sun Ray group's noted weaknesses in its attempts to develop a reference client base for its novel computing solution.

Demotivation Is Contagious (and Affects Even Those without the Traumatic Experience)

At a critical moment in the Sun Ray product launch, the JavaStation merger with the Sun Ray group brought two teams together that until then had been fierce competitors. Some antipathy was sure to result that was not beneficial for the integration of the two teams. But more importantly, it brought together a team that had recently undergone the traumatic JavaStation experience with a team that had not.

As one member of the Sun Ray team recalled, people moving from the JavaStation team brought along "a culture of failure" to the Sun Ray team that had finessed an intimate working style resembling an ambitious start-up. Every Monday morning, for example, the Sun Ray team had been holding a meeting during which plans for the week were collegially discussed and problems addressed in real time. This style of working was no longer possible after the team suddenly became 10 times its prior size. Thus the merger was not only disruptive in (lack of entrepreneurial) spirit, but it also forced a change in the working routines of the group that now had to decide how to take advantage of the many more (and perhaps less focused) people on its team.

As evidenced in our interviews, these changes caused feelings of trauma in the Sun Ray team. Thus, trauma can travel (see Barsade, 2002;

Czarniawska & Joerges, 1996; Westman & Etzion, 1995). The exceptional experience of Sun's famed engineering department's not delivering in the case of the JavaStation was transferred to the perceptions of the Sun Ray as untrustworthy: guilty by association. It is important to shape the perceptual context of an innovation in such a way that such contagion does not readily occur.

TREATING INNOVATION TRAUMA (AND BUILDING RESILIENCE)

What can organizations do, then, to treat traumatic experiences from innovation failure so as to maximize learning for future projects? How to build resilience from experience?

First, related literature from organizational change indicates that individuals need time and opportunity to disengage from past experiences (Nadler, 1988). Directly moving the remnants of the JavaStation group into the Sun Ray project allowed no time for dealing with innovation trauma and loaded the Sun Ray group with unnecessary emotional baggage. By the same token, the Sun Ray team should probably have done more to disassociate itself from the legacy of the JavaStation team—an act that became difficult after the merger of the two teams but that could still have been possible due to the different technology platforms and large turnover in the composition of the team.

Second, postmortem workshops on the underlying causes can help create a common understanding of the course of events that led to the failure. This, in turn, may assist individuals' rationalization of what happened and why. Often the cause of the failure is not straightforward (Bartunek, Gordon, & Weathersby, 1983), as in the case of the Sun Ray, thus adding to the complexity of the experience. Was it the nature of the product (technology?) that caused the innovation not to live up to the expectations, or was the project management at fault in its less-than-optimal market development? Or was it simply too late to upset Microsoft's monopoly? What should (or could) have been done differently? (As Jay Moldenhauer-Salazar of Sun's HR Labs and I conducted our interview research on the Sun Ray case, we felt occasionally like therapists helping people to heal a wound and make sense of the experience in retrospect, from a distance.) Was my performance at fault? To what extent is someone or something else (for example, the management or the timing of the product launch) to blame? Was it all JavaStation's fault?

Third, collaborative case writing can be used by team members to avoid trauma by maximizing learning from failure. In this method, companies systematically write their own cases, that is, cooperatively document the knowledge and experience they themselves have acquired (for example, Probst, 2002). Traditionally, case studies are mostly used for teaching purposes in management training (Locke & Brazelton, 1997; Thomas, 1998). Through conveying intricate problems and experience, they are uniquely suited for portraying the tacit knowledge and experience acquired over time. Not only do tacit best practices and common experiences become explicit, but new light is also shed on past failures, disclosing important lessons learned. Moreover, this learning can be situated in the larger context of a company's technology and innovation strategy, where a project failure marks a setback rather than a definitive and ultimate blow to long-term success. An internal Sun Ray case has been used in Sun Microsystems' Leadership Institute, in part, for this purpose.

Fourth, innovation trauma can be alleviated by carefully managing the excitement for a new project. For example, avoid overloading the project with unrealistic expectations. The company expected to sell 100,000 Sun Ray machines the first year. The much lower actual sales were an early (and perhaps unnecessary) signal of failure. The hype shifts expectations and invites trauma by creating conditions that are overwhelming; in that case, people often feel unable to exercise any control (for example, Stuart, 1996). For example, the extent to which such a discrepancy between expectations and outcomes is perceived as threatening to one's career in the company (Hogan, 1987) may determine the degree of the trauma experience.[5]

Fifth, the perception of losing control over the development of the highly vested project in a critical moment can be traumatizing (Greenberger & Strasser, 1986). The JavaStation merger was an event that led to the founder team losing control over the project at a very critical point in development: just before the expected product launch. Also, the roller coaster of changing executive sponsors contributed to the team's feeling of not being in control of the Sun Ray's destiny while adding to the burden of trying to position and shape the product so that it would fit within the current sponsoring business unit's strategy. Thus more stability in the management structure would have likely given a sense of being (more) in control to the team, something that would have likely eliminated some potential for emotional hardship (Bandura, 1977).

ABOUT THE CASE STUDY

Some years ago, Jay Moldenhauer-Salazar, then a director at Sun's HR Labs, and I (with the help of Sun's CTO Greg Papadopoulos) identified the Sun Ray as a "potential radical innovation" within Sun, a product that was outside of Sun's existing portfolio, that had the potential to shift industry paradigms, and yet had not lived up to sales forecasts. Thus we were interested in the Sun Ray both as a success story—its ability as a radical idea to survive into a product and to continue as a Sun product throughout a dramatic economic downturn—as well as its failure to live up to expectations. We hoped to understand the factors that enabled the Sun Ray's stubborn survival as well as the factors that prevented it from becoming "the next Java" (a common catchphrase at Sun).

To understand the Sun Ray's story, we interviewed—often multiple times—nearly 40 people central to that story. We took careful notes of the interviews, which were analyzed with the help of volunteer research assistants from Sun's HR organization. Indeed, we were confident after these interviews that we had spoken with every person who played a significant role in shaping the Sun Ray into what it has become today. We also compiled nearly 300 documents, from internal memos to market analyses to press releases to meeting minutes. These documents helped us sort out fact from fiction as conflicting tales emerged from the interviews in workshops to which we invited our most dedicated research assistants to participate in the triangulation of data. In all, our fact finding spanned nearly a year, including the validation of the facts in the case write-up with every interview participant. Finally, we studied the case through different interpretative lenses to gain a richer picture (March, Sproull, & Tamuz, 1991), and we wrote an analysis of the study through each perspective (Moldenhauer-Salazar & Välikangas, 2008).

PAST PERFORMANCE AS A THREAT TO RESILIENCE

Strategic resilience, as a reminder, is the capability to turn threats into opportunities prior to their becoming either. Past performance is the enemy of such astuteness. High success seduces people to believe there are no threats to them (could not possibly be, and even if there were, they were plenty capable of handling them). Mediocre performance just does not care as long as the organizational life can be continued comfortably (from their perspective). Mediocrity also likes to ignore the chance that extraordinary or outlier events can happen because mediocrity's experience does not suggest the events (the lack of such trying or stretching experience often defines mediocrity). Very low performance has no time to observe anything other than its own internal machinations. Far-away threats are of no consequence in the struggle for survival now.

COMPLACENCY

High performance: Reckless belief in self; assured of superiority (highly exposed)

Mediocre performance: Lack of ambition; maintaining the status quo

Low performance: Rigidity resulting from threat; inward focus (failure trap)

IN A STATE OF ARRESTED DECAY

I am writing this book in Virginia Lakes, which is 25 miles from Bodie, an old gold mining town in the Eastern Sierras between the towns of Bridgeport and Lee Vining, California. Left intact after its residents abandoned the town after two bad fires and its gold reserves dwindling, Bodie is now a true ghost town. The houses still have their furnishings and belongings just as they did when it was a busy center of 10,000 people. One of California's largest towns in the 1880s, it will now be left to turn to dust as it is worn away by the summer heat and winter snow.

Walking around Bodie and peeking into the buildings still standing, like the Bodie hotel ("Meals served at all times") and the school (a little girl, perhaps a student there, is famed for writing: "Good-bye, God. I am going to Bodie."), gives you an eerie feeling of times gone by. But you can also sense that those days were vivid, full of life (lots of whiskey drinking and shooting evidently included) and gold mining, of course.

Bodie is a great analogy for many corporations—the state of its maintenance is called "arrested decay." The California parks department does not seek to repair Bodie but simply tries to slow down its eventual demise—supporting a house wall with a log to keep it from falling or closing a door blown open in the wind to protect the insides (see photo). Perhaps arrested decay is what many once successful companies find themselves in—hoping to prolong the worn-out glory for visitors to witness as long as possible.

Photograph by Jaak Treiman (August 2009)

DIFFERENTIATING SUCCESS FROM SURVIVABILITY

It is important to remember to differentiate success from survivability. Many people living in developing countries have developed innovative strategies for survival that may not be successful in any conventional meaning of the term, yet are highly survivable. Similarly, companies that currently enjoy record performance may wish to inquire about the sources of this success: how sustainable and adaptive are they? Success tends to induce belief in the continuity of favorable circumstances and develop trust in the capacity to react in time and cope with environmental jolts or sudden economic shifts. Yet this may be undeserved if it is not yet tested. It is often said that the resilient organizations should enjoy and even search for hard times as they are the ones to benefit.

"A company is successful until it is not." The end of success almost always comes as a surprise (it comes after denial and blaming momentary circumstances). AT&T blamed its arch rival's marketing campaign for the declining cost of long-distance telephony in the 1990s even though the cost had been declining since World War II (see the case study in Chapter 8). By the time the company no longer is successful, it is costly to take corrective action, and survival may be at risk. (AT&T was acquired by SBC, one of the baby bells, although the merged company kept the AT&T corporate name due to its remaining brand value.) Like the ghost town of Bodie, many once very successful companies, failing to differentiate success from survivability, manage to maintain only a state of arrested decay (see the sidebar vignette "In a State of Arrested Decay").

To survive beyond (the most commendable) bouts of success, it is necessary to build resilience. That is the topic of Part Three.

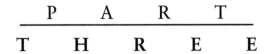

PART

THREE

STEP 2. BUILDING RESILIENCE INTO THE ORGANIZATION

Strategic resilience is a capability to take serendipitous, opportune action. It is reminiscent of Karl Weick's (2000) assertion that "reliability is a dynamic non-event"—constant attention is required to prevent a disaster or an accident. The difficulty of building strategic resilience is that we do not know where the next turn of events will come from; therefore, writing an emergency action plan is not sufficient.

Resilience capability is not a specific enemy. It is not a specific management function. It is not a defined task. It is not a hierarchy of responsibility. It is not business development. It is not a growth strategy. It is unlikely to be found in any formal documents or rules. Instead, it is what the CEO of a very successful U.S. company described: "If I knew where the next challenge will come from, I would be able to defend against it. But it is the challenge I cannot anticipate, that we need grassroots resilience capability for."

Perhaps a tempting way to define strategic resilience is to follow Potter Stewart's statement about defining pornography, made when he was an associate justice of the U.S. Supreme Court: "I know it when I see it." It is obvious in retrospect. But the question is, how to build such capability *before* you need it, while you still have time to develop it—beyond staying alert, taking a different route home every day (avoiding routine), communicating with people who are farther away in your network (for lucky serendipity), and "expecting the unexpected." Building an arch when it is not (yet) pouring.

Through a number of case studies, in this part I set forth key building blocks for making organizations as resilient as possible. These building blocks include organizational intelligence, resourcing, robustness (or design), and adaptiveness. The embedded case studies illustrate these factors in action. Finally, I discuss resilience as inner strength—something the Finns call *sisu*—that is at the core of any kind of resilient effort or culture. We begin, however, with the consideration of leadership.

WHY LEADERSHIP MATTERS, BUT IT IS NOT SUFFICIENT

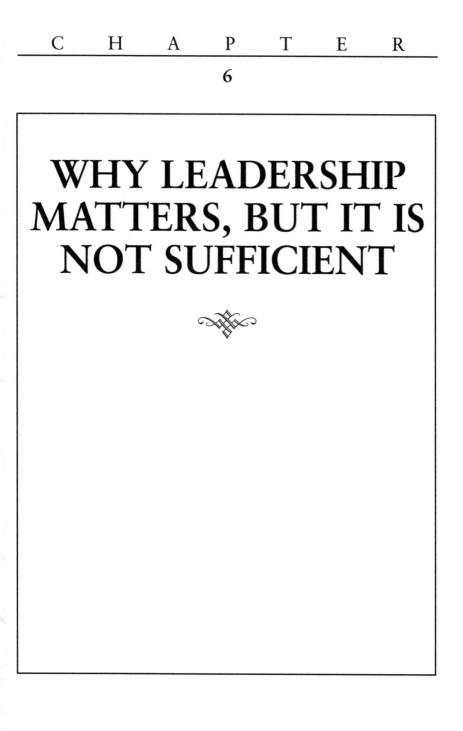

A standard response to any human or organizational shortcoming is a clarion call for better leadership. Sure, leadership can always be improved upon. As leaders, we are particularly susceptible to notions of self-efficacy ("I can handle this") and the escalation of commitment ("I cannot be seen making a 180-degree turn because it will detract from my credibility as a leader").

Our thinking on present issues also tends to follow that of prior decisions: The prior meeting's agenda provides a basis for the current meeting's discussion and thus creates tunnel vision. We learn more and more about a narrower and narrower area, or as Jim March, student emeritus of organizations, says: We improve ourselves to obsolescence. Our past experience shapes priorities—what we know of and are good at must be (by definition) important. These familiar, comfortable areas then easily drive out the exploration of new, potentially emergent, opportunities. Thus the organization becomes managed by its leaders' comfort zones, not by strategic intent or opportunity discovery, and it can easily find itself stuck in situations that were not part of any strategic plan.

INCREMENTALLY COMMITTED[1]

Strategic Commitment Is Often Less an Act of Leadership than It Is a Result of Incremental Decision Making

In Stanley Kubrick's beloved movie *Dr. Strangelove, or: How I Learned to Stop Worrying and Love the Bomb*, a U.S. Air Force general orders a nuclear strike against the Soviet Union only to find out that the Soviets have devised a doomsday device that—if attacked—will end all human life. This was meant to be the ultimate deterrent. The problem was that the military had not announced the existence of such a weapon to the world!

(continued)

Stranger things happen in the corporate world. In our research of commitments entered into incrementally, my colleague Armi Temmes at the Helsinki School of Economics and I have found multiple examples of strategic binds, lock-in situations, or path dependencies that are unforeseen outcomes of decision streams. Sometimes companies end up stuck, like a Finnish design company that was at the mercy of a monopsony (only one customer) in its biggest foreign market having committed to an exclusive representation; sometimes companies get lucky as in the case of Honda's well-known entry into the U.S. car market (Pascale, 1984). No matter the ending—unfortunate or fortuitous—both the design company and Honda exhibited incremental strategic choices made without the full appreciation for the consequences (Mintzberg & Waters, 1985). We call this phenomenon *commitment creep*: a no-return situation created through cumulative decisions, often by multiple organizational actors. Such commitment creep typically emerges from the company's leadership, but it can occasionally be used deliberately to create a certain desired outcome.

Such an example of the deliberate use of commitment creep is reported by Bower and Gilbert (2007): a corporate division had managed to build an entire plant without requests for capital expenditure by breaking the work orders into small enough portions to escape corporate control. But the chimney was too large to be built under radar; thus a request for a capital project proposal was put in. By the time the controller received the chimney request, the entire plant (minus the chimney) was already there. What was there to do but to grant permission for the chimney, hoping that the plant would be a good investment (which it evidently turned out to be)?

Explanations of Commitment Creep

The phenomenon of commitment creep is not by any means absent from the literature of strategic management. There are a number of theory perspectives that speak to it in some way (see Table 6.1 for a summary). The desire to appear consistent as a leader may perpetuate a course of action even when it is clearly doomed (Staw & Ross, 1987). Perhaps not surprisingly, companies tend to change course by changing leaders. Gist (1987) suggests that self-efficacy may produce overconfidence and result in feelings of invulnerability or excessive optimism, thus leading to the escalation of actions (Whyte, Saks, & Hook, 1997). March and Shapira (1987) suggest that the managers' tendency to pay more attention to the risk of loss than to the risk of missing a possible gain (see also Thaler, Tversky, Kahneman, & Schwartz, 1997) may induce passivity—and creeping external events may then take their course in creating unforeseen binds.

Table 6.1 Explaining Commitment Creep

	Individual	**Organizational**
Deliberate	• Self-efficacy • Managerial attention • Risk aversity	• Premium on leadership consistency
Emergent	• Decision-making heuristics • Cognitive myopia	• Escalation of commitment • Organizational learning • Competency traps • Structural inertia and organizational routines • Strategic momentum • Founding conditions and imprinting forces

Simon (1947), March and Simon (1958), and more recently Ocasio (1997) have emphasized the limits to human cognition. Time-constrained managers do have to constantly make choices about what to pay attention to, as time does not afford consideration of all matters (Ocasio, 1997). Thus the perpetuation of a particular course of action may be a simple result of the selective intake of information, chosen on the basis of the current strategy. During the course of a busy day, paying attention to emerging or intervening issues not previously on the agenda may be difficult (or perceived a luxury the manager can ill afford).

(*continued*)

There are a number of heuristics that govern busy everyday judgment. Such heuristics help managers make shortcuts based on prior experience and quick evaluations of a situation (for example, Hoffman & Ocasio, 2001; Newell & Simon, 1972; Lau & Redlawsk, 2001; Keats, 1991). Experiments by Tversky and Kahneman (1986) have shown that thinking is easily anchored to a matter that may have little relevance to the eventual judgment, simply by the fact of its being mentioned. And studies show that acquired attitudes may not change even in the face of strong contradictory facts (Barr, Stimpert, & Huff, 1992). The cognitive framing of the issue persists. Levinthal and March (1993) have called attention to a number of such examples of cognitive myopia, which—as by-products of learning—often act as traps. For example, it is tempting to focus one's attention on a familiar area and ignore less familiar ones, even if those others become increasingly salient to the matter at hand, while one's own narrow competency becomes more and more irrelevant (Levitt & March, 1988; March, 1991). It's like constantly improving your English when what's really needed in today's global business environment is Mandarin.

There are also organizational (or possibly institutional) explanations of commitment creep. The escalation literature is an analysis of the factors driving the ever-deeper commitment. There may be sunk costs, political reasons, and/or ideological or cultural norms that make a turnaround difficult if not impossible (Staw & Ross, 1987; Ross & Staw, 1993; Brockner, 1992). The project may become perceptually inseparable from the success of the institution. Or the change in course (or admittance of failure) may mean significant loss of prestige, organizationally and individually. Or the shift may be difficult to justify if current practices serve existing customers and stakeholders well: Christensen (1997) describes the dilemma incumbents face in responding to disruptive technologies, ending up losing business despite making managerially defensible decisions at any one point in time.

Commitment Creep: Implications for Resilience

Organizational actions that accumulate into strategic outcomes over time can render a company in unforeseeable trouble. Such commitment creep presents a threat that strategy outcomes will turn out to be quite different from what had been planned, and they will emerge outside top management's vision or control. A CEO may, to his or her surprise, find past operational-seeming actions have locked the company in a particular strategy that is difficult or costly to reverse and change. A European steel company found itself heavily dependent on one of the key raw materials for making stainless steel while the commodity prices for that material were rising aggressively. While this affected all steelmakers equally, the very high cost slowed down the core business significantly as stainless steel became relatively expensive compared to other available materials. The organization had become unintentionally and unknowingly committed to a less-than-optimal strategy.

While there are always surprises—not all turns of fate can ever be accounted for—a resilient company will systematically evaluate the potential outcomes of its strategic and routine decisions combined, and like the steel company, turn a threat into an opportunity by using the eventuality to make the company much more imaginative and stronger for the future.

THE BURDEN OF LEADERSHIP

Leadership is a political act, and it must earn, for its effectiveness, followers' willingness. Resilience cannot be commanded. The leader must make the case for investing in resilience, and thus build the political will. This can be difficult when there are other, urgent issues on a daily basis such as paying the bills or shipping the goods out. The cost of reform may be large and immediate, while the benefits let us wait for them.

It is often not clear that the people paying the cost for resilience are the ones that benefit from it the most. The most vulnerable people may be the most exposed yet the least able to pay. Bangladesh, one of the world's poorest countries and home to 154 million people, is likely to disappear due to global warming, as a tragic case in point. The *New York Times* has reported (September 8, 2009) that Kenya has been subject to the worst drought in decades, as rains have again failed and "lush land dries up."

Further, coordinated action is clearly necessary to respond effectively to global warming, yet difficult to mount since one person's effort to reduce his or her carbon footprint makes no difference if other people continue to act as before. There is a temptation to take a "free ride." If the majority of people change their behavior, everyone, also the free riders, will benefit. Yet those who change pay the direct cost, and the rest of us get the goods free. This can erode morale and hence any motivation for collective action.

Also, sometimes persisting in a pursuit may be tough precisely because it *is* working, thus reducing the perceived need for continuation (for example, if there is no visible threat). These are tough challenges for resilience leadership. Regardless, tough but foreseeable challenges are the very burden of leadership.

THE DIFFICULTY OF TAKING ACTION

Hurricane Katrina was "one of the most fully predictable and scenario-tested nature disasters in American history, but that fact still did not lead to appropriate preparatory actions or adequate crisis response on the part of the responsible officials at the local, state, or federal levels" (Fukuyama, 2007: 3). Thus leadership failed at all levels of government. Explaining that "obviously the wrong people were in charge" (sic!) is too simplistic an explanation. Where were the "right" people and what were they doing?

THE PERILS OF TAKING COLLECTIVE ACTION

- Mounting political will (Not me. Or, Why now?)
- Overcoming denial (Can't be happening.)
- Catalyzing sufficient action to make a difference (the majority or an influential minority)
- Managing cost versus benefit distribution (over time)
- Preempting free riding (Otherwise the collective will to act may erode.)
- Persisting in the pursuit (against time and a perceptible lack of threat)

The truly unforeseeable, rare events also plague us. Such black swans may have catastrophic consequences. One such event would be a large asteroid hitting the earth, which might end life on earth upon collision. Another example would be a financial meltdown of the scale just experienced, with lots of risks hiding under the surface that were not detected, or acted upon, in time by the public that was to pay for the eventual consequences in tax dollars. And the accumulated effects of past decisions that suddenly create large-scale systemic change: we can no longer expect the past risk ratios to hold.

The burden of leadership is such that it is wise to bet on resilience, not on leadership alone. Build resilience into the organization. It is necessary because of the likelihood that leadership actions will be delayed, wrong, inadequate, or just missing. (Perhaps the wrong person was indeed in charge!) Building resilience into the organization improves the company's chances to survive the moments of weak leadership and to get through (eventually inevitable) strategy shifts. Resilience is what organizations can fall on, when leadership fails.

ORGANIZATIONAL IDEATIVENESS

Idea exploration is an important strategy for the future. Ideation allows us, with very little cost, to explore different development paths and scenarios. Ideation invites playfulness—going beyond the boundaries of everyday expectations. Resilience thus raises the question: how *ideative* is your company? How many idea people do you have thinking for you? Ideativeness has little to do with brainstorming sessions. Rather, it is about the capacity to think of the future in different and sometimes radical ways. Whether these ways are good or bad, desirable or not, matters little. Thinking about them and talking about them builds resilience. As a leader, you will then not be coldly surprised. Remember the old strategist's truth: it is not the plan; it is the planning that makes you prepared. (Or, "No plan survives contact with the enemy.")

MAKING RESILIENCE A NATURAL ACCOMPANIMENT TO THE ORGANIZATIONAL DAY

Therefore, I propose making the organization—rather than its leadership—resilient. Instead of relying solely on the leader's capacity (whether it's a CEO or a head of government) to take preemptive or corrective action in time, the organization should be imbued with resilience capability. Such resilience building still requires some intention and determination on everyone's part (including the leader), but when resilience is a natural accompaniment to organizational activities, it becomes everyone's responsibility. Also, turning threats into opportunities on a daily basis is much more effective (and perhaps continuously rewarding) than doing so when the corporation is at the end of its success run. Such continuous action also makes resilience a real-life, everyday capability rather than an abstract concept that is to be invoked at the times of crisis. When the crisis hits, it is not at all given that the resilience capability is there to be galvanized, unless it has been frequently enough rehearsed. (It is like assuming that you can outrun the tiger, should the need arise, without testing the matter ahead of time, before encountering the very tiger you ought to be running away from. Well, not many people live to tell their success story.) It is good to battle train before the battle.

Resilience building concerns five dimensions that make strong and imaginative organizations: organizational intelligence, resourcing, design, adaptation, and culture (or *sisu*, a Finnish word suggesting tenacity):

1. *Organizational intelligence:* Organizations are intelligent when they successfully accommodate multiple voices and diverse thought.
2. *Resourcing:* Organizations are resourceful when they manage to mitigate change or even better, use resource scarcity for innovative breakthroughs.
3. *Design:* Organizations are robustly designed when their structural characteristics support resilience and avoid systemic traps.
4. *Adaptation:* Organizations are adaptive and fit when they rehearse change.

5. *Culture:* Organizations express resilience in a culture when they have *sisu*—values that do not allow the organization to give up or give in but instead invite its members to rise to the challenge.

Let us consider how to build resilience in each of the five organizational dimensions in turn.

Organizational Intelligence: Resilience as Imaginative Thinking

The guiding principle for organizational intelligence from the perspective of resilience is inspired by the classical Ashby's *law of requisite variety.*[2] As the law states, the capacity to accommodate environmental change depends on the variety available inside the organization. Weick (1976) talks about the "cultural insurance" that affords the multitude of interpretations inside an organization. Cherish the conversation with different voices and perspectives! Have framing contests (or interpretational debates of what's going on) for important strategic issues. How does the opportunity frontier change? Requisite thinking ought to express as much possibility as contained in the environment (and hopefully little more). Only highly imaginative thinking inside the organization can accommodate such thinking outside. (Not all people with imagination work for one company either!) Therefore, from the resilience point of view, the key is not integration and alignment of the executive team or organizational members in general—such characteristics may be good for smooth and fast execution. From the resilience point of view, it is the variety and imaginativeness, reflective of environmental threats and opportunities, that are critical for organizational intelligence. Such requisite thinking can be enhanced by the following:

1. The ability to act under ambiguity (when you are not sure about the right answer)
2. Never taking your own (ready) answers for granted (Always keep examining them: are they self-serving?)
3. Questioning the received setting in which the problem and the solution are formulated: under whose authority, following which

decision-making routines, is the issue framed? Invite framing contests and strategy debates.

4. Add thinking redundancy/equifinality/ambiguity (multiple meanings) through one of the following methods:

   - Playing devil's advocate (Someone acts as a challenger to consensus decisions.)
   - A shadow executive team (a group of junior organizational members who express their views on strategic decisions for discussion with the "real" executive team)
   - Developing a network of independent people to entertain contrasting and differing views about future scenarios
   - Maintaining "hypocrisy": Keep talk and action separate to allow the organization to cope with inconsistent societal demands that cannot be reconciled [Brunsson, 1996 (in Warglien & Masuch, 1996)].
   - Use humor, or even a "corporate jester," to make points that otherwise would be rejected (see the Chapter 8 sidebar, "A Note on Jesters and the Role of Humor"). Jesters are, by their function and through their antics, able to make occasionally true and helpful (maybe annoying) points that others would get fired for.

5. Explore the issue in terms of extremes (grotesque, for example): What is the very best or worst possible case? What is still possible (even if unthinkable in its consequences)?

6. Consider the expected outcomes of important decisions, and write the outcomes down at the time of the decision making.[3] Compare the events that unfolded to the expected course of events. What does the difference suggest about the decision assumptions?

Schwartz and Randall [2007: 97–98 (in Fukuyama, 2007)], in their discussion on anticipating strategic surprises, recommend being "both imaginative and systematic." Beyond raw labor, it is important to have the knack to put together different bits of information in a way that builds various scenarios and event paths. Thus, one must be able to consider serendipity as part of one's calculation in such a way that it enhances the interpretation of what can be (made) possible. This is being "serendipitously sagacious." One may be able to be lucky and wise and identify an opportunity as per chance.

WHAT IF . . .?

Roman children played with a toy called an *aeolipile*, made up of a metal ball suspended by pins on each side so that it could spin freely; the water-filled ball had directional nozzles on the top and bottom. When the water in the ball was heated, steam would jet out and spin the ball. The aeolipile was, in short, a rudimentary steam engine. Imagine if some innovative Roman had envisioned this child's toy enlarged and hooked to a set of wheels moving under its own power on the Appian Way. As it happened, there was no such Roman. [Bonvillian (in Fukuyama, 2007: 70)]

Imaginative thinking must also be able to cope with issues that are possible but are also, by their nature, unthinkable. Perhaps their consequences would be horrendous. Or, from our own perspective, undertaking such action would be madness. Or we prefer not to see the slow erosion of our company position in the marketplace due to competitor action. After all, the final consequences will not be seen for many years to come, and they may not be so bad anyway. Hope vacates judgment. (Or we simply decide to leave the issue for subsequent managers and generations to deal with.) By definition, we are in denial over such issues (unless we are simply being calculative—*not a problem during* my *tenure*). The faster we get over the denial, the sooner we can begin to deal with the issue.

In the long term, said Keynes, we are all dead, and thus no more capable of fixing things.

RESOURCEFUL, ROBUST, AND ADAPTIVE: THE BUILDING BLOCKS OF ORGANIZATIONAL RESILIENCE

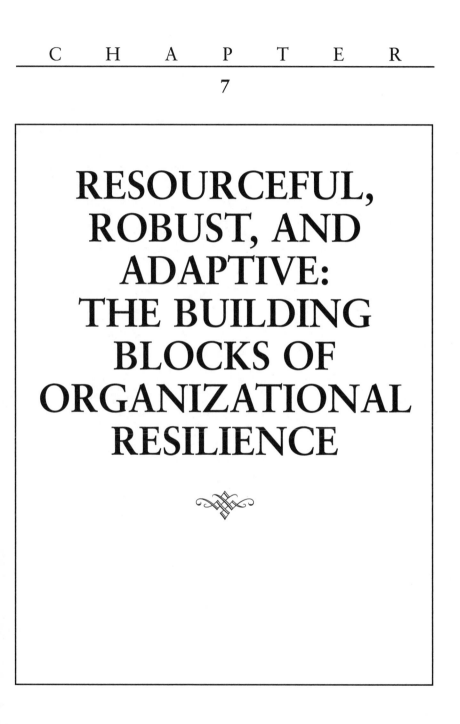

How do you build organizational resilience beyond the leadership's capability? The defining dimensions are resourcefulness, robustness, and adaptiveness. This chapter considers each issue in turn and describes strategies that will enhance such organizational resilience. Sometimes the most useful strategy may be counterintuitive—rather than hoarding resources for a safety cushion, perhaps the resilient response is to use a resource constraint as a catalyst to develop an innovation capability.

ORGANIZATIONAL RESOURCEFULNESS: RESILIENCE AS INNOVATION

> If I were not so convinced of your Highness's integrity, I should imagine that you wished to gamble with the King of France's forces without having any of your own, to see at no risk what would happen.
> —Liddell Hart (1968: 99)

How much do you need for a rainy day? This is the traditional question of resilience. Illustrative are the recent calls for raising capital ratios in banks that had fallen from 10:1 in the 1970s to 73.7:1 by 2008 (Ferguson, 2009). This indicates very high leverage, which was a highly beneficial position when the wealth creation strategy was working well. But when the strategy failed, the financial crisis exposed a severe lack of resilience. It had been recommended, for instance, that "precautionary reserves" be increased "not in the ratio of the volume of business, but in the square root of that ratio" (Olivera, 1971: 1095).

High resource leverage—using resources to their maximum capacity and beyond—has often been seen as smart business. Such high leverage has been seen to drive innovation, noticeably in the financial industry. Interestingly,

Hagel, Brown, and Davison (2009) have found that corporate returns on assets (ROA) in the United States have, since 1965, dropped drastically. Cost savings may be competed away, as the authors suggest, or the leverage strategy is causing a lack of resilience that penalizes companies over time. Clearly, a rethink is needed.

Mitigation of Risk

One way to mitigate risk is to have reserves. Savings help us cover any unexpected expenses. Most governments maintain oil reserves in case of supply disruptions. Military reserves that can be called upon in a crisis may provide a feeling of national security. Resilience is often interpreted as a sort of mental reserve—the capacity to draw strength from at times of crisis. Family and friends help here too.

Organizational reserves are basic building blocks for collective efforts where the harnessing of human effort together is needed. For example, Germany has a strong middle-sized company sector (so-called *mittelstand* companies); and the Silicon Valley in California is vibrant in entrepreneurial reserves: founding of companies and pursuing emergent business opportunities in high technology. South Korea has its *chaebol*: large corporations that have dominated particular industries for decades. France has its national champions. Whether these organizational reserves provide resilience for a country or region in question depends on their capabilities to turn threats into opportunities. Nevertheless, they constitute the collective reserves these countries naturally depend on in times of crisis. (Witness Nicolas Sarkozy's and Angela Merkel's 2008 responses to the financial crisis in France and Germany, seeking to ensure the viability of their incumbent companies and business models—emphasizing the role of public institutions in France and export industries in Germany.)

Redundancy

Airplanes have multiple landing systems. People have two kidneys. Companies use double-entry accounting systems. We are advised to think twice before embarking on a venture. Most people have two parents. DNA is a double helix.

We have only one head though—perhaps that is because otherwise, no one would know who is in charge. (And therein may lie one of our weaknesses—no team decision making to challenge our potential biases). Our brains are highly redundant, though, and generally capable of compensating for a lost functionality.

CHARACTERISTICS AND TYPES OF REDUNDANCY

- Repetitive
- Spare or twin
  - Replacement
  - Substitute
  - Mirroring
- Instantly reproducible or copyable
- Obvious
- Unnecessary
- Ambiguous (with multiple meanings or interpretations)

The lack of redundancy exposes a potential vulnerability: Liddel Hart (1968: 159) criticizes the Japanese in the Russo-Japanese war for failing to take advantage of the Russian war effort's being "entirely dependent on a single line of railway—the Trans-Siberian." No redundancy there, though the enemy failed to exploit it.

The resource redundancy approach can of course be criticized for its slack, and therefore less-than-optimal, efficiency. Idle resources (or investments just in case), though not productive in the traditional sense, can be interpreted as having value, as security blankets or stepping stones. The value is in their ability to mitigate and buffer against risk, provided that they can be called upon as needed. This assumes certain stability in the case of a security option or flexibility (or liquidity) (see the vignette sidebar "Real-Options Reasoning for Resilience"). Reserves may, of course, also act as a deterrent: your being able to afford a good lawyer may reduce your opponent's willingness to sue, or a country's having a large army capable of defense may decrease its enemy's eagerness to attack.

REAL-OPTIONS REASONING FOR RESILIENCE

Real-options reasoning suggests that options have value in limiting the exposure to downside events (and thereby provide a source of resilience). They thus allow for more activities of discovery commonly prone to failure such as entrepreneuring (McGrath, 1997, 1999). Options are a way to hedge against uncertainties in the competitive environment. As shortcuts to a possible action or a loss limit, options have value independently of whether any one option is eventually followed through on or not.

Innovating through Resource Scarcity

A grand alternative to relying on reserves against unexpected events is a competence I call *resource-scarce innovation* (Gibbert, Hoegl, & Välikangas, 2007). Its essence is captured in the old saying, "Necessity is the mother of invention." Resource-scarce innovation breaks through problems by finding solutions that require radically less (or different) resource usage than before. This is in contrast to the prevailing orthodoxy which suggests that problems that are slow to solve may require additional resourcing.

In actuality, the resource shortage is propelling the push to innovation. For example, an R&D project may require more time or more staff to be completed. This may be true in some cases, but the presumption is that the problem must be solved within the existing operating or thinking framework. Such a resource-driven mindset (Hoegl, Gibbert, & Mazursky, 2008) easily foregoes the opportunity of finding entrepreneurial or innovative solutions (Starr & MacMillan, 1990) at much lower resourcing levels. Such resource efficiency, then again, is likely to add to the resilience of the corporation by way of making do with less—or lowering its fixed costs.

Please note that this efficiency, or making do with less, is not a matter of leverage, as discussed before. This is resilience that stems from human ingenuity or entrepreneurship: it is about solving the problem with a different determination. Resource-scarce innovation breaks out of the framing that the issue could be solved only if a little more were invested. Rather, solutions are teased out by *changing* the assumptions. For example, instead of cutting costs by 10 percent, try solving the problem by cutting costs by 90 percent or more. This is what is currently happening in places like India (see Prahalad, 2004). Of course, a technological innovation may also change the resource constraints, such as the use of a hybrid engine in a car.

Sometimes the very act of resource-scarce innovation is also an act of resilience: for example, using a shovel, a poor person's only tool, as a frying pan at the end of the day. The poor person carefully cleans the shovel and now uses it for cooking the evening meal.[1] Or consider another example, seen in Guguletu, a township near Cape Town, South Africa: residents use old cola and beer cans to build temperature-resistant houses to shelter people from heat and cold. In China, the repairers of Haier, China's largest appliance maker, discovered that small farmers used their washing machines not only to launder clothes but also to clean vegetables. The repairers relayed this user innovation to product managers, who in turn asked engineers to install wider drain pipes that would not clog with soil and grit. The manufacturer also affixed large stickers to the modified machines with instructions on how to wash vegetables safely. By marketing this innovation and others—including a washing machine optimized to make goat's milk cheese—Haier effectively spread a resourceful innovation among entrepreneurial farmers in rural China. In the process, Haier also won market leadership in China's rural provinces (see Sull, 2005).

CONSTRAINTS SPARK CREATIVITY[2]
Coauthored with Michael Gibbert and Martin Hoegl

Constraints, especially resource constraints (of which there are plenty in an economic downturn), are key to innovation. Think of them as boundaries that incite creativity. In fact, that is how many designers work: the consensus is that the more the constraints, the better the outcome!

Let's step back in a time of heavy resource constraints and consider, for instance, the Messerschmitt *Kabinenrollers* (cabin scooters), which were developed by one Fritz Fend, an aircraft engineer, and produced in the factory of the German aircraft manufacturer Messerschmitt in the

(continued)

1950s and early 1960s, a time when German aircraft manufacturers weren't allowed to build planes. Incidentally, Messerschmitt was also the first company to produce a fighter jet [along with Heinckel (see Gibbert, Hoegl, & Välikangas, 2007)], so it is probably no surprise that the *Kabinenroller* looked like a scraped-off fighter-plane canopy on wheels (of which there were, appropriately, only three). More to the point, this "at-hand" kind of thinking led to characteristics such as aircraft light-weight materials, tandem seating, and aerodynamic styling, which made the little car not only highly fuel efficient—even by modern standards (87 miles per gallon or 2.7 liters per 100 kilometers)—but also very fast for its day (65 miles per hour or 105 kilometers per hour).

Or consider another fuel-efficient microcar that was built more than half a century ago: BMW's Isetta. The origins of this car were with the Italian firm of Iso SpA. In the early 1950s, the company was building refrigerators, motor scooters, and small three-wheeled trucks. Iso's owner, Renzo Rivolta, decided he would like to build a small car for mass consumption. By 1952 the engineers Ermenegildo Preti and Pierluigi Raggi had designed a small car that used the scooter engine, and they named it Isetta—an Italian diminutive meaning "little Iso." It is said that the stylists had arrived at the award-winning design of the Isetta by taking two scooters, placing them side by side, and adding a refrigerator door!

ORGANIZATIONAL ROBUSTNESS: RESILIENCE AS A DESIGN ISSUE

When designing systems that are resilient, robustness is called for. Robustness is the system's (or organization's) structural stability to survive challenge while maintaining operability (and reliability). The more varied and intense the challenges the organization can cope with, the more robust it is. Robustness is also the capacity to accommodate multiple, different futures [being a "multimission" organization (see Levchuk, Meirina, Levchuk, Pattipati, & Kleiman, 2001)]. In this sense, robustness is the port-folio of strategies available for an organization and its capacity to adapt to or resist change to negotiate its future. Robustness can thus be structural (a return to stability) or strategic (dynamically adaptive) in quality.[3]

Structural Robustness

Structural robustness is the ability to survive challenge and maintain form. The key to structural robustness is to avoid systemic risks materializing and collapsing the organization. Beyond solid operations, such structural robustness can be enforced through loose organizational coupling: different organizational parts occasionally communicate but do not depend on each other for operability. Thus the organization (or some of its parts) tends to remain functional longer under stress as damage can be more easily isolated. Modularity, or organizational design that can be broken into separate independent parts, similarly adds to robustness but also to flexibility as one part can be replaced without other parts being affected. (Note that robustness is an important operational resilience concept in crisis management, and as such, it is outside the focus of his book.)

TAGUCHI AND ROBUSTNESS

A Japanese engineer, G. Taguchi, greatly influenced the robustness of quality control and experimental design in the 1980s and 1990s. Taguchi suggested that "quality" should be thought of not as a product being inside or outside of specifications but as the variation from the target. He was concerned not only with the understanding of product but also with societal quality costs that would ultimately, he thought, find their way for the corporation to pay. Taguchi's methods pertain to the design and the manufacturing of a product. Taguchi claimed that making products insensitive to process variations was often cheaper than controlling the causes of such variation (Taguchi, 1986, 1987). See Levchuk et al. (2001).

Strategic Robustness

Strategic robustness is the ability to accommodate change in a timely, nontraumatic way. It is a dynamic capability that can be judged only over time as a response to competitive challenges. To master strategic robustness, the managerial tasks are the following (Hamel & Välikangas, 2003: 54):

> *The cognitive challenge:* A company must become entirely free of denial, nostalgia, and arrogance. It must be deeply conscious of what's changing and perpetually willing to consider how those changes are likely to affect its current success.

> *The strategic challenge:* Resilience requires alternatives as well as awareness—the ability to create a plethora of new options as compelling alternatives to dying strategies.

> *The political challenge:* An organization must be able to divert resources from yesterday's products and programs to tomorrow's. This doesn't mean funding flights of fancy; it means building an ability to support a broad portfolio of breakout experiments with the necessary capital and talent.

> *The ideological challenge:* Few organizations question the doctrine of optimization. But optimizing a business model that is slowly becoming irrelevant can't secure a company's future. If renewal is to become continuous and opportunity driven, rather than episodic and crisis driven, companies will need to embrace a creed that extends beyond operational excellence and flawless execution.

Mastering the cognitive, strategic, political, and ideological aspects of management increases the company's capability in strategic renewal that is forward looking rather than crisis prompted. Such renewal capability cannot be isolated to any one part of the organization but must be the responsibility of the CEO and everyone else.

Behavioral Robustness

Finally, robustness has interesting behavioral dimensions (or perhaps tendencies to gain power). Padgett & Ansell (1993) study Cosimo de' Medici and his rise to power and control of Firenze during Renaissance: "The Medicean political control was produced by means of network disjunctures within the elite, which the Medici alone spanned" (p. 1259). It took Cosimo a while to realize this potential of his network, though (p. 1264). However, Padgett and Ansell also speak of the multiplicity of behavioral motives that allowed

Medici to claim action to be in the city's interests while benefiting his own purposes. Such ambiguity allowed that "everything was done in a response to a flow of requests that, somehow or other, 'just so happened' to serve Cosimo's extremely multiple interests" (p. 1263). Being able to entertain such a grand number of varied interests is kind of robust accomplishment in itself; yet the key to behavioral robustness here is the multivocality—"the fact that single actions can be interpreted coherently from multiple perspectives simultaneously, the fact that single actions can be moves in many games at once, and the fact that public and private motivations cannot be parsed" (p. 1263). Thus it is crucial for robust action "not to pursue any specific goals" (p. 1264) or lock the organization into the pursuit of a particular goal in case of change. "Victory, in Florence, in chess, or in *go* means locking in others, but not yourself, to goal-oriented sequences of strategic play that become predictable thereby" (p. 1264). Robust behavior is keeping the options open while making it difficult to discern one's ultimate motives—selfish or otherwise—for any particular move.

ROBUST ORGANIZATIONAL DESIGN

Type of Robustness	Static Representation	Dynamic Representation
Structural	Modularity	Loose coupling
Strategic	Portfolio of options	Adaptive managerial capability (cognitive, strategic, political, and ideological challenges)
Behavioral	Idiosyncratic network	Multivocality (goals and interests)

ORGANIZATIONAL ADAPTATION: RESILIENCE AS A FITNESS ISSUE

Organizations seek purposefully to better "fit" their environment (that is, have a competitive, profitable business). Researchers differ whether such adaptive intentions are effective: strategic management theorists typically claim timely change as the primary management goal; population ecologists suggest that this is unlikely and organizations should focus on what they do best, reliably. Stick to their knitting rather than seek to change with the times. Natural selection then decides which organizations can survive (or have market demand). This may, as presupposed, be economically efficient, yet the CEO and the employees must then of course try to get new jobs (which may be occasionally fine too). This calculation however leaves open the costs of corporate failure. (Yet everyone agrees that the most expensive alternative has the ineffective corporations continuing to operate suboptimally indefinitely, and not failing.)

Vulnerabilities of Change

At stake is what it costs to change including how much this changing creates distraction in the running of the business. In a well-known framework, March (1991) juxtaposes exploitation—the capacity to focus on core business—with exploration—the capacity to create something new. Presumably, exploration carries a cost, while exploitation brings in the revenue.

A case in point, BP, the British energy company, recently reversed course from renewable energy ("beyond petroleum") back to its core oil and gas business. The new CEO, Tony Hayward, suggested in the *Financial Times* (July 8, 2009: 7) that somehow the company "had lost track of" its business fundamentals—that is, what it is good at: "finding oil: high-cost investments that can create big increases in value" (according to a former BP executive). BP had invested substantially in renewable energy during the former CEO Lord Browne's tenure; yet the effort now appeared like a distraction to operational safety. BP's until-then stellar reputation suffered from a number of industrial accidents.

Arguments for Change
- Survival depends on responding to changes in the marketplace.
- It is important to be proactive.
- By changing, a company may be able to avoid obsolescence.
- Change is fun and helps decrease the boredom of routine.

Arguments against Change
- Any change introduces elements that are new and hence potentially risky.
- Changes tend to take the focus away from the core business or "job number 1" and thus become distractions.
- There is only so much change any organization can accomplish at any one time.
- There is resistance to change—and even rejection or fear of it.

To overcome the syndrome of change (and innovation) being a costly distraction, there are a few imperatives. One is to manage the exploration of the new. This involves the creation of small-scale experiments that can be run outside the mainstream management systems and learned from (see the Chapter 9 case study for examples).

The second imperative is to build on already-existing change seeds in the company. There are likely many different ideas and initiatives in the organization even if some of them are underground. Burgelman (1983) speaks of always-existing autonomous behavior in organizations—grassroots activism that cannot be suppressed but can sometimes force adaptation of the corporate strategy to be inclusive of the potential opportunity. He uses the descriptive concept "strategic forcing" to illustrate this struggle between the old and new: strategic forcing is about making the old accommodate the new, somewhat (but not totally) changing the strategy.

The third imperative is to cultivate cognitive frames that allow the consideration of the existing situation in different perspectives. Such considerations may open up new strategic avenues and uncover so-far-unthought-of options. In some organizations, such framing contests (Kaplan, 2008) take place routinely; yet it is important to ensure that the competitive frames are simply not minor variations of each other but instead present genuinely different ways of looking at an issue. One way to examine this is to ask: What opportunities open up if this problem of framing, rather than that one, is adopted? In other words, what if we see the business challenge as an aging of our customer base versus an opportunity to enter senior care? This is a matter of perspective, and it is probably the cheapest, if sometimes the hardest, form of change.

However, the ultimate in adaptive fitness is to be in better shape than is required for the race at hand. Such resilience build-up is particularly necessary as change rarely comes from the exact direction we expect it from, and it rarely delivers the results hoped for in the time scale aspired to. It may, however, surprise us with its force much later. The Chapter 9 case study explains how to build such reservoirs for change while the company is still highly successful. Anticipating certain challenges and preparing for them is one thing; the more challenging aspect of resilience is to be ready for emergent challenges coming our way. Having resilience in change, no matter what content, duration, or direction that change may take, is about building resilience even beyond those changes that have been correctly anticipated.

Being resilient means making turns even when the road forward still looks passable. It is like going to the gym: you do it (partly for fun but in particular) to stay fit and build the "change muscles" should they be needed.

SISU: RESILIENCE AS INNER STRENGTH

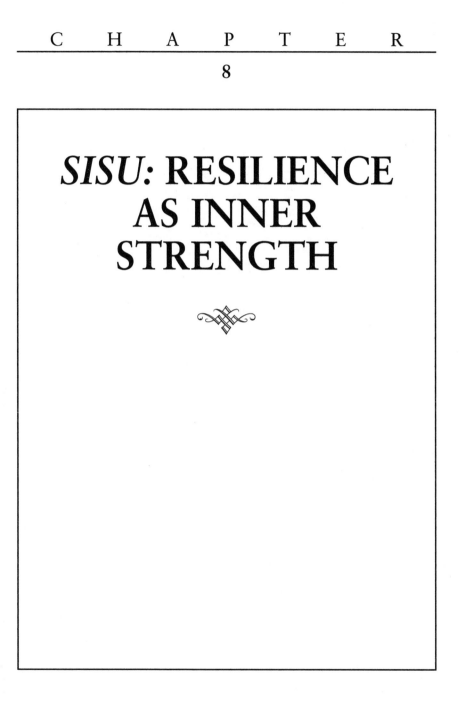

The word *sisu*[1] denotes, in Finnish, a certain tenacity, persistence, and toughness, perhaps even hardheadedness, in the face of adversity. It is a personal (or national) quality, one that may be necessary to survive in the latitudes of the far North, having fought wars with much bigger neighbors and learning to respect the fragile yet tenacious nature that gives nothing for free. Sitting in the shade under a mango tree and waiting for the fresh fruit to drop down for eating would not constitute a very viable life strategy. The Finnish national literature tells tales of frost killing the year's only harvest as a standard plot line. As one Estonian refugee (also a daughter of harsh climate and political conditions) who traveled via Helsinki, Stockholm, and Sidney in the 1940s and 1950s to become a successful businessperson in the United States, now in her nineties, declared when asked about the hardships of escaping, with a newborn baby, Estonia under Soviet occupation during World War II: "Give up? There is no such option." There is a soul of steel.

I have found *sisu* in many parts of the world: not only in the Northern countries but also in many others including Afghanistan. The case study of Innovation Democracy below tells an Afghan story. *Sisu* is formative as Innovation Democracy has self-funded its operations and has sought to break away from the traditions of development aid. The limitations of such aid, and its tragic lacking of impact, have been lamented by people such as U.S. Secretary of State Hillary Clinton in March 2009. As recently as my December 2006 experience in a Kabul home, despite billion-dollar aid, Kabul still had electricity only an hour or two a day. Afghans have developed their own small-scale innovation to help: I saw old car engines converted into electricity generators in an effort to provide warmth in the winter. While this causes some pollution, the innovation points to power solutions that are modular—focusing on the needs of the single family unit—and that are portable and potentially more effective than building the large centralized infrastructures still only in the planning phase.

Tough conditions require innovative solutions and *sisu*, elements that Innovation Democracy seeks to bolster. I believe that resource-driven thinking has so dominated development aid that it has clouded considerations of situations in which, paradoxically, scarce resources (precisely because they are scarce) are effective,[2] potentially leading to breakthrough innovations and lasting alleviation of poverty. I suggest supporting emergent local innovation and entrepreneurship as a means to help Afghanis improve their living standards and develop a more stable society. Let us start by identifying the portfolio of ideas and activities that Afghan people are passionate about. Let us fund these ventures first. Top-down financial aid reduces if not voids the incentives to find innovative solutions to overcoming the underlying, true resource constraints. It also builds resource dependency (if you think power corrupts in government, try free money!)—an enemy of resilient development and of *sisu*. The issue is important beyond development: similarly in the climate negotiations, billions of dollars of climate aid are now committed by governments. If we do not know how to spend monies to reduce poverty, how do we quickly learn to transfer monies wisely across nations to slow down global warming?

RESILIENCE IN ACTION: INNOVATION DEMOCRACY, INC.

Innovation Democracy, a California nonprofit organization, founded by Sari Stenfors, Jaak Treiman, and Liisa Välikangas, supports local innovation in countries important to world stability. With a determined Afghan woman, Wagma Mohmand, the organization has operated in Afghanistan for five years, teaching the students of Kabul University's Economics Department innovative entrepreneurship. More than a course, the program is an engagement with the students to help them develop means to support themselves and their families in an extremely difficult, resource-poor, and occasionally hostile environment. Upon its founding in 2005, the vision of Innovation Democracy, Inc., was formulated as follows:

> Yes, we aspire to save the world. Not by big capital expenditures or large-scale aid. *By taking small actions and turning them into significant beginnings.*

Mission 1: Make the ability to contribute—and innovate—everyone's right and privilege in a society.

Mission 2: Invigorate people's belief in their own self-worth. Boost and support their capacity to make a difference to their local community and beyond.

Mission 3: Find innovative ideas and people already working on local initiatives to turn their novel ideas into business ventures. Act as an experienced mentor and early-stage investor in ingenuity and entrepreneurship.

Our philosophy holds that change efforts and change outcomes are often asymmetric—small interventions can produce large results not by scaling but by compounding the effort. *Sisu* is thus needed to maintain the grassroots quality or micronature of the effort in all its diversity and richness. (It is tempting, but very damaging, to go for the one-silver-bullet solution.) Consequently, we have a number of beliefs regarding development aid that are rather unorthodox relative to the common standard as to how such aid is given. Rather than paying for foreign consultants to come and develop plans for improvement, we support the efforts of local people to find their own—however modest—solutions.

OUR PHILOSOPHY: SMALL BEGINNINGS; COMPOUNDING CHANGE

Myth
Big outcomes require big investments.

Our Conviction
Small, well-timed, and innovative acts are the levers of transformational changes that accrue over time.

Myth
Social progress trickles down from policymakers to individuals.

Our Conviction
Grassroots profit-motivated initiatives produce self-perpetuating returns to the society and economy.

(continued)

Myth
The underprivileged or the unfortunate require aid, not investment.

Our Conviction
Investing in people is a long-term venture, not a momentary act of charity, and its returns often benefit the children of those now in need.

During the yearlong program of Innovative Entrepreneurship at Kabul University, the students learn practical business skills, including the writing of a business plan. In addition to market research, the students work as apprentices in local companies. The participation teaches *sisu* because the program is demanding (and is extracurricular and thus invites participation entirely on a voluntary basis). As opposed to rote learning common in Afghanistan, the Innovative Entrepreneurship Program teaches imaginative, critical thinking, group work skills, initiative, and promptness. It also offers new role models (the teacher is an accomplished Afghan woman, and the class is visited by many local entrepreneurs). Modernizing education, cultivating habits of inquiry, and curing the imagination deficit (by means of a learning journey to the organic farms in Northern California, for example) are key to finding solutions to persisting problems locally.

We also believe that the students of the Innovative Entrepreneurship Program will play a critical role in eventually stabilizing the society in Afghanistan. They are the "best and brightest" as graduates of Afghanistan's premier university. Helping them to build a good life for themselves and their families will give the graduates an interest in the stability and prosperity of their society. As the talent of their society, they have a multiplying factor that far exceeds anyone else's. Their efforts carry consequences. Such impacts are built bottom up: What other powers cannot dictate with large development aid budgets, grassroots efforts can build with resilience, taking a few steps forward even if there is an occasional step backward. But at least the graduates are taking the steps themselves—they have ownership of their chosen path of resilience. Resilience cannot be built but by the efforts of those whom these efforts seek to benefit—and that requires learning *sisu*—both from those who provide it and those who enjoy the benefits.

EXTREME INNOVATION

A way to exercise *sisu* during more peaceful times is to practice *extreme innovation*—that is, a way to escape the incremental and go to the extreme of what is possible. Extreme innovation is also innovation in extreme conditions. Such a (return) visit to the frontier edge can help people understand the ultimate consequences of particular actions and help them come to terms with perhaps unlikely but still possible outcomes. Beyond a real trip to a place like Afghanistan to test one's survival capacity, extreme innovation means exploring what is absolutely the best and/or worst case or simply the most-out-there possibility or occurrence of the phenomenon of interest.

Extreme innovation means breaking away from incrementalism—going far beyond the linear increment or improvement. Strategies for extreme innovation include following a particular path to its logical end to see its extreme or final consequences, exploring the phenomenon through its possible grotesque manifestation[3] (like caricatures in cartoons), and finding the *outlier*—the person or event that is as far from the average as possible.

Try to find an innovative solution to the problem in extremely resource scarce conditions. These extreme examples can be good ways of finding out one's tolerance limits and hence test one's *sisu*. Sometimes a *jester*, a person whose function is to poke fun or make comments that are so true no one else could state them, is needed, as explained in the section "Corporate Jesters."

Some strategies for practicing extreme innovation:

- Visit either a place where people live on virtually nothing or otherwise a place that has very tough conditions.
- Consider the grotesque (cartoons do this in the form of a caricature).
- Determine what is (logically) the final case if the path suggested is followed.
- Find the outlier—the case that is as far out there as possible.
- Study the problem in extremely resource scarce conditions—how would you solve it there?
- Employ a jester (see the section "Corporate Jesters").

CORPORATE JESTERS

One of the factors aiding (and perhaps also testing) *sisu* and hence resilience is humor.[4] A corporate jester is one way to exercise extreme innovation with humor. A jester may challenge the orthodoxy, ridicule convention, and test the ultimate faith of people and their (perhaps mistaken or otherwise self-important) ideas. Jesters may thus act as important messengers for resilience in particular when we are overly obsessed with an idea "that refuses to leave us" or we are overcome with our own power.

A NOTE ON JESTERS AND THE ROLE OF HUMOR

In "Of Managers, Ideas, and Jesters,"[5] Guje Sevón and I argue that ideas are very resilient—indeed more so than people who often succumb to their persuasion. Humor is important to combat bad ideas that do not go away or that reappear in history again and again.

Managers, and humans more generally, occasionally become imprisoned by the idea of personal success—for example, exhibiting strong cognitive inertia even when faced with the necessity of change (Kets de Vries, 1990; Tripsas & Giovanni, 2000). Signs of ideas ruling over managers include persistence with obsolete strategies or competitive notions (Barr, Stimpert, & Huff, 1992); an obsession with a particular (faddish) management technique, such as total quality management (TQM) (Backstrom, 1999); and the act of engaging in gross misbehavior or brutality in the name of an idea or a cause (see, for example, Huntington, 1996).

We suggest that a jester is a unique social institution that evolved to help humans cope with the ideas that refuse to leave them. A jester is a tradition dating back to medieval times that counterbalances, as one of its important functions, the power that ideas hold over us through a unique privilege, the freedom of (humorous and witty) speech. Anything that a jester would say was "in jest" or an "utterance of a fool," thus seemingly discounted (yet still effective). A fool has many names: *buffoon, clown, minstrel*.[6] Klapp wrote in 1949:

> The fool is a symbol of fundamental importance, representing a role
> especially valued by the group. The fool is a social type found widely
> in folklore, literature, and drama (p. 157).

Jesters mediate the historical battle of power between ideas and humans [and this is one of the reasons for their universal prominence as an institution in human history (see Otto, 2001)]. The mediation is particularly visible in the case of court jesters and kings. To be able to jest, the first step is to remind the king of the fragility of his position. The jester "becomes the person who through various means reminds the leader of the transience of power. He becomes the guardian of reality, and in a paradoxical way, prevents the pursuit of foolish action" (Kets de Vries, 1990: 757). The jester is thus a useful antidote for the persuasions of power that tend, over time, to diminish a person's ability to judge his or her own performance and capabilities objectively (Kets de Vries, 2003).

Thus it is in companies also. The role of the jester, first and foremost, implies the right and skill to make people to see themselves and their actions more clearly. Paul Birch, now a former British Airways' corporate jester, has been quoted as saying: "Fools pinpoint absurdity by acting out the absurd. They act as a mirror in which people see their mistakes without having to admit to them. This enables Fools to challenge accepted wisdom and create new alternatives. As such, they're entrusted with the sensitive task of managing and controlling change."[7] A jester can thus be a key player, the master interpreter, in the power struggle for the definition of the firm's strategy, for example. Kaplan (2004) has documented strategy making as such a framing contest—a battle of whose view will prevail in directing the firm's future. The function of a jester, and that of humor more generally, is that of an aid to such contesting, familiar in the courts of kings. It can also be important in corporate strategy making.

A jester may be a role, played by someone like Paul Birch at British Airways, or it can be the frequent collective referencing to a cartoon like Adam Scott's *Dilbert* in corporate presentations. A jester may be an outside consultant too. But jestering is an important social institution we should recognize. Many people my coauthor Guje Sevón and I have talked with claim themselves to be jesters in corporate life. Thus we should include jestership in our accounts of organizations and leadership not only because such jestery is probably common but also because one of its distinct benefits is that it is one of the few defense mechanisms humans, and managers, have against the power of possessive, sometimes obsolete, occasionally dangerous and destructive, ideas.

A jester's ability to mediate between ideas and humans stems from the privileges of being a fool (Otto, 2001). Only fools (and perhaps children as in emperor's missing clothes) can be forgiven the unique privilege, without demolishing the social order, to point out the (too) obvious, the forbidden, and the partially hidden. Jesters can make the ideas that embody us and that we perform, sometimes unknowingly, visible. A jester facilitates the undressing of such masquerades. A good jester's wit then also serves as a lubricant to the reckoning. The nakedness that would be rejected offhand, were it not coated with humor, now becomes more palatable. There is less denial. And the hold of ideas on us diminishes with our laughing at ourselves.

The humorous absurdity or incongruity of it all eventually shifts perceptions (Polimeni & Reiss, 2006). "The fool breaks down the boundary between chaos and order, but he also violates our assumptions that the boundary was where we thought it was and that it had the character we thought it had" (Willeford, 1969: 39). The jester may thus aid the accomplishment of cognitive innovation—a breakthrough or a breakout of the ideas that normally characterize or dominate our thinking. This breaking out of ideas can be collective too: the use of humor has been found helpful in navigating contentious situations in corporations (Hatch, 1997) while shared laughter communicates ease or nonthreat (Ramachandran, 1998).

A jester can be a potentially powerful agent of change, enhancing the organizational ability to escape obsolete or misguided ideas and absurd orthodoxies. Of course, jesters can also work toward maintaining the status quo. A jester can act as a social controller, by ridiculing those who profess heresy or are outsiders (Klapp, 1962). So choose your jesters carefully, so that they too will not become possessed by the undue persuasions of too powerful ideas. Humanity's actions can sometimes be inexplicable in their dark consequences—perhaps ideas then rule over humans. Jesters can help build resilience against such ideas.

CASE STUDY: RESILIENCE IN ACTION—BUILDING RESERVOIRS FOR CHANGE

Since its founding in the early 1980s, the company had grown fast to reach a prominent position as one of the most successful consumer retailers in the United States. Despite occasional hiccups related to double-digit annual growth, the company had consistently outperformed its competition. Its CEO, however, felt challenged by the past success that set the investor expectations beyond the status quo. The notion of resilience—that is, the capacity to adapt to change in a timely manner (before the need for change becomes "desperately obvious") and without first having to undergo a potentially traumatic and costly crisis (Hamel & Välikangas, 2003)— appealed to him, as he had read the referenced article. In November 2004, he stated that his challenge was to ensure that the company would continue to be successful, even if such a continued success is rare in corporate history. He saw resilience as offering a potential avenue to tackle the odds.

The company thus embarked on a "quest for resilience" in December 2004. First, as a diagnostic step and in an effort to initiate discussion about specific resilience impediments, 21 managers were interviewed about their views on impediments to resilience at the company. The questions ranged from open-ended ones such as, "What do you believe today potentially impedes the company's ability to effectively respond to change?" to specific questions about cognitive, strategic, organizational, and other barriers to strategic renewal in their area of responsibility. The responses were eventually summarized and represented as a Barrier Wall—a set of Legolike bricks that had a specific barrier written on each brick, forming an impediment cluster by color. (See the sidebar "Resilience Impediments: A Summary" for the barrier categories.) The representation became one of the inputs for a resilience enhancement workshop called the Management Innovation Jam, as described in the next section.

RESILIENCE IMPEDIMENTS: A SUMMARY

- Bureaucratic sense of responsibility
- Standardization: One size fits all
- Human nature: Personal fear, mistrust, and cynicism
- Inflexible policies and processes
- Don't know how to drive change

The next experimentation phase began with the formation of a small team to motivate and explore the effort. Most of the work was performed on a volunteer basis. For example, there was a team of eight people from different parts of the company who together designed an exhibition that was to become a key communication tool. Called the Resilience Deficiency Ward, the exhibition featured small beds with pillows that had names of once leading retailers embroidered on them. The point was to invite the 4,000 people (including the company board of directors) who visited the "Resilience Hospital" to ponder the temporariness of success and analyze the causes that brought these leading companies to the brink of extinction. Does their own company suffer from any of these resilience deficiency symptoms? was the question each visitor to the hospital, wearing a lab coat and reading the "X-rays" that described the malaise of the hospitalized companies, then answered. The exhibit's purpose was to engage participants in the diagnosis of resilience but also to motivate participation in the quest on the grounds of a personal, memorable experience.

The exhibit visit was the kickoff to a workshop that came to be known as the Management Innovation Jam, an opportunity to innovate the company management principles, processes, and practices so that one or more of the resilience impediments could be removed. The jam invited the participants—some 30 to 50 volunteer managers and employees at any one event—to consider the following: (1) the impediments to resilience at the company; (2) resilience principles extracted from such adaptive systems as cities, markets, and democracies; (3) examples of management innovation from nonconformistic settings (such as the novel formation of editorial rights of a Web site called Slashdot); and (4) ways to apply the resilience principles and examples so that one or more novel ways of accomplishing managerial work can be created (for example, an internal marketplace for ideas and talent). The jam ended with encouragement to develop an experimentable design for the management innovation idea and try it out on a small scale, without causing disturbance to the mainstream management system. There were no formal endorsements of the ideas and/or experiments, and there were no formal resources allocated to their experimentation. However, given that a few of the participants held a senior position in the company, some teams had access to company resources through their discretionary budgets. Other teams simply donated their own time, working through lunch or early mornings, in addition to their regular jobs, and they sought to benefit from available slack resources the best they could.

Two Management Innovation Jams were held in the spring of 2005, one in March (which the CEO attended as a gesture of support and to speak to the group on the importance of resilience to the company) and the other one in April (attended by the COO who also was supportive of the quest). During the jams and thereafter, management innovation ideas were advanced as experiments by self-formed teams that had developed the initial idea and were motivated to take it forward as an experiment. As a result, a portfolio of management innovation ideas was formed. The sidebar "Some Experimental Management Innovations" provides some examples of the ideas advanced.[1]

SOME EXPERIMENTAL MANAGEMENT INNOVATIONS

- *eBay for Human Capital:* A marketplace for matching ideas and talent across the company
- *The Idea Reserve:* A place to find a mentor or a "personal idea banker"
- *The TagWiki:* An open-communication and community-building platform
- *The Red Dragon:* A technology platform for harnessing innovative ideas
- *The Boss's Boss's Learning Journey:* Taking the manager to whom your manager reports to, to visit a place that both of you would find instructional and enlightening

During 2005, the volunteer community, known as Jampions (having attended a Management Innovation Jam and being champions of resilience and management innovation), grew to 250 people (of which all except 10 directors or above were managers or employees). The community began to hold themed monthly Resilience Clinics as regular get-togethers and discussion forums. Teams of Jampions presented their ongoing experiments but also invited outsiders to talk about related work (such as customer service experiments ongoing in stores). An internal resilience Web site was set up that invited anyone to become familiar with the notion of resilience and join the quest.

Most active Jampions joined the ongoing effort to further develop the content for the Management Innovation Jam, to make it experiential and easy to relate to. They also helped to redesign the jam from the original two-day event to a one-day event. They then participated as facilitators and mentors to new Jampions, sharing some of their experiences as management innovators. Some new material was developed, including a play on resilience (where a number of Jampions had leading acting roles) and an inspirational video that showcased "the resilience principles" and issued an invitation to the audience: "Join the quest for resilience. Become a management innovator." Videos were also developed based on interviews with existing Jampions, describing their management innovation ideas and experiments, and these videos were used in addition to the Jampions attending and participating in multiple forums in person. The forums included hosted discussion groups on the challenges of innovation. Groups of Jampions met with the senior executive in their area of responsibility to share their insights and give the senior executive a chance to ask questions and offer support. In November 2005, a group of senior executives, including the CFO, were asked to present their perspectives on resilience in a roundtable discussion with the Jampion community.

Additional activities included an Idea Elaboration Jam, a workshop to support the experimentation of ideas and to develop them as experimental, iterative designs that benefited from some of the test methodology used in the company in its retail stores. Case studies were also written about other company change programs in the past, offering some potential learning in how to engage in organization-wide change. There were regular informal conversations about whether the company manifested any of the "resilience deficiency" symptoms common to companies in the Resilience Hospital (such as complacency or lack of effective strategy options when the retail environment changed). A reading list and resilience glossary were produced together with a manifesto.

The final period began in November 2005 when the company hired a new executive (in a position of a COO) to cut down bloated administrative costs, which had gained attention by industry analysts and had taken a toll on the quarterly profit. Despite various appeals by Jampions on the importance and the low cost of the work they were doing, the quest for resilience was one of the programs cut as part of an overall blanket effort to trim the number of activities ongoing in the company. Nevertheless, the program left a lasting impact. To quote one of the number of similar e-mails received by the program lead at the time:

> Thank you for driving this journey. I greatly admire your creativity and passion you brought to this initiative. Through the tools and support you provided, I've been able to network with other people within [the company], experiment with management innovation, and mentally engage in work differently.
>
> Even though the Resiliency Journey has reached its conclusion, please know you've made a difference with the hundreds of Jampions you've connected together. I believe [the company] is better because of it.

WHENCE RESERVOIRS FOR RESILIENCE?

What immediate and lasting effects might the program have created in the company and for the participants? Let us first consider what tends to stand in the way of resilient change—that is, the issues that were found to be impediments as revealed in the company interviews, and how the program eventually helped participants begin to address these issues and facilitate learning as spillovers to other activities.

Mental Models and Precommitments

Beyond complacency as a seductive companion to success, received mental models frequently act as impediments to adaptation, requiring the unlearning of past truths (Argyris & Schon, 1978). Rationalizing issues away, mistaking luck for smarts in explanations of success, and having difficulty admitting that current strategies may be decaying were some of the perceived impediments related to dominant mental models.

The visit that over 4,000 people made to the Resilience Deficiency Ward (or Resilience Hospital) was instrumental in a realization that successful companies eventually (or abruptly) fail too. The discussion that followed regarding the "resilience deficiency symptoms" that their own company may be exhibiting allowed further reflection along these lines: "The other retailers, now in the Resilience Hospital, also had smart people like us working there. But they did not do enough. . . . They allowed themselves to be complacent. . . . They did not see the signs for change." Thus, as a result of the exhibit visit and follow-up discussions, there was among the participants an emergent recognition of the temporariness or fragility of success. The playfulness of the experience allowed a discussion that might not otherwise have been possible.

Routine Behaviors

Overconfidence in business as usual is one of the adaptive barriers that is constantly rehearsed within the core business of the company. The counterpart barrier is then the lack of experience in the exploration of novel areas, crowded out by business routines. The routine business feels easy and confident; exploring anything new seems difficult and intimidating. Thus the lack of *rehearsal* of necessary new explorative behaviors becomes an impediment to change. To quote one participant: "If we don't exercise the 'change muscle' now, we won't have it at our disposal during future setbacks." Rehearsing change serves the same purpose as going regularly to the gym: to be in good shape as a company for future challenges.

The need for rehearsal, or the practicing, of change was observed in other ways too. The fear of failure was one strong manifestation. The nomenclature of experimentation invited frequent discussion: "What if the project fails?" (which is OK because it is "only" an experiment); and "How do we know this [experimental idea] is *the* solution?" (which we do not; that is why we are experimenting). Experimentation thus enabled the rehearsal of change, without the necessity of avoiding a perceived failure at any cost.

Lack of Available Options

A common challenge to companies facing disruptive strategies by their competitors is that they lack any effective responses (Christensen, 1997). Similarly, it is probably difficult to create truly novel management innovations. Thus managers tend to refer to and copy so-called best practices (what other companies are doing) as solutions to their management problems. At the extreme, this becomes the search for a silver-bullet solution. Such a quick fix can be rolled out effectively, but it will ultimately fail to solve the underlying issue.

This company tendency was combated in the program by participants deliberately seeking to develop multiple solutions to persistent problems (such as the harnessing of innovative ideas companywide) and experimenting on the ideas on a small scale and iteratively. Thus participants discovered ways to resist the temptation to rush into a large-scale implementation of a definitive "pilot" without first understanding the idea's implications and its conditions for effectiveness.

The Portfolio of Management Experiments

The management innovations were independent, autonomous initiatives with dedicated teams. At any one time, there were some three to five management experiments being tried. Though often on a small scale, they produced learning about what was possible to accomplish in terms of management innovation ("no permission required to do this experiment in the front of the company café"). While none of the experiments has been directly adopted as mainstream management methods, they did provide important insights into resource allocation, idea harvesting, motivation, and innovation management, such as people being willing to volunteer their time to projects they consider important for the company's survival or for the sake of their own careers.

The Jampion Experience and Consequent Activity

Ten Jampions formally reflected on the program impact. In the interviews by a neutral party in August 2005, the Jampions commented on their experience as a Jampion, how it had changed the way they work or think about their work, and the responsibilities they may have acquired since becoming Jampions. A typical statement was one that suggested the Jampions' willingness to experiment on new ideas more than before and see them in a broader context or not to dismiss ideas offhand based on preconceived notions. Many noted that they now approached their own work differently—daring to question standard approaches and consider alternative work strategies. According to one Jampion, the physical experience gave him new courage—no amount of abstract thinking would have accomplished the same.

Jampions also frequently discussed their pioneering role in the Resilience Clinics. The discussion typically touched on the question, "How do I behave as a Jampion role model to others?" Many people felt they were part of a cause that they had chosen to join because it felt important to them and gave meaning to their everyday work. They *sought* opportunities for resilience-enhancing behaviors, such as the application of the experimental approach in their work tasks or a conversation with a peer about how they would "know if the company had become resilient." These and other activities led to a number of outcomes 6 to 12 months later; for example, some of the Jampions founded a spinoff independent company whose purpose was to find ways to enhance employee work-life balance in large corporations. Also, a community program that started as part of one of the experimental initiatives was later recognized by the CEO in the corporate social responsibility report as an important example of employee activism. A few other business-related ventures followed.

Finally, the Jampions took what they learned and applied it in other work. For example, another, unrelated, project dealing with the role of women in the company made use of the management innovation and experimentation tools developed in the project to advance the women's cause accordingly. Also, a management innovation idea (a prediction market for holiday gift cards) emerged outside the jams as one manager was exposed to the approach and sought to develop an early management innovation of his own. This initiative continues to evolve in the company.

PRACTICING CHANGE

The *capacity* for resilience is proposed here as something that is built through rehearsal, or the *practice*, of change. Such an activity reservoir is perhaps not unlike slack in an organization, enabling innovation when necessary (Cyert & March, 1963). The perspective offers a way in which the practice of change can be assessed as to its resilience value. The reservoirs for resilience may be evaluated, to begin with, by asking: Did a substantial number of people become mobilized and personally committed, individually and in teams? Did community members develop ways to be inventively experimental in their activity, to innovate and to experiment? Did community members become mindful beyond the focal activity? Did community members gain personal courage to question the status quo? Did they apply the lessons they learned in other work tasks?

These questions stem from the understanding of resilience as something requiring broad contribution from volunteer innovators contributing their diverse perspectives to the quest rather than relying on a CEO's privileged viewpoint alone. While it is not clear that the management innovations embarked on were the right ones should the environment change, the benefit was the practicing of an experimental process that can be repurposed to provide future management innovations as needed. Thus resilience in this case was learning a problem-solving methodology rather than a single solution.

What is needed is *practicing* change rather than waiting until change becomes a necessity. If unrehearsed, the exploration of the new will probably be unnecessarily difficult and ultimately not very successful: like going to war without battle training. While many companies spend a lot of intellectual energy in strategizing, they may forgo the practicing of change—how to implement any eventual strategy. Both are certainly needed, and resilience is likely to reside in the generative dance between what is known and what can be done.

CASE STUDY: IMAGINATIVE THINKING IN ACTION—THE CASE OF THE ODDSTERS AT AT&T

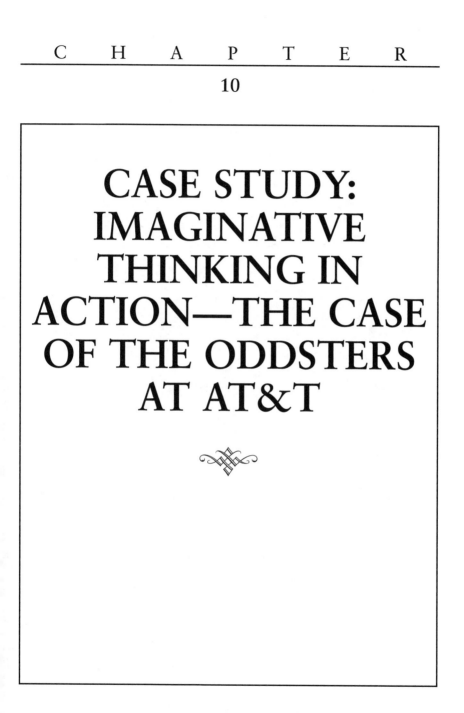

The following case study, which I coauthored with Amy Muller, is an example of highly imaginative thinking in a once revered organization. It also illustrates some elements of corporate jestering as the scientists—the main players of the case study from AT&T Labs—called themselves ODDsters for the Opportunity Discovery Department and occasionally left others wondering.

THE LIFE AND TIMES OF ODD: THE ODD MISSION AT AT&T[1]

The one thing most managers are sure about is that scientists cannot—and should not—meddle in corporate strategy. For heaven's sake, they know nothing about business! And yet this is a story about how a group of scientists within AT&T—then the leading long-distance provider in the United States—proved them wrong. This is a story of rare corporate spirit on one hand, and management failure on another. The sting is that even a group of this caliber—some of the smartest people from Bell Labs who have enjoyed renowned careers since—could not reverse AT&T's decade-long failure to adapt to a hostile environment, replete with new competitors and disruptive technologies.

Starting in 1995 and lasting through early 1998, AT&T's Opportunity Discovery Department (ODD) was a hotbed of just the kind of heresy that could have given the company another chance. Nestled in a corner of the AT&T Labs[2] in Murray Hill, New Jersey, ODD comprised a group of eight energetic souls who, for three and a half years, devoted their considerable talents to the salvation of AT&T.

Like many good ideas, ODD was conceived around the proverbial water cooler. Its four founders constituted an eclectic assortment of researchers led by Greg Blonder, an MIT and Harvard–educated physicist who directed AT&T's Customer Expectations Research Laboratory and also served as AT&T's chief technology advisor. ODD's mission—at least, its nominal mission—was to help AT&T make smart choices in the allocation of its enormous research and development budget. For most of its 100-plus year history, AT&T, through its famed Bell Labs, and by virtue of its monopoly status, had dictated the technological future of networks. But with new competition and disruptive technologies looming, AT&T Bell Labs was no longer in charge. It was time for a forward-looking view of technology strategy—one that recognized the existence of other players in the new world.

As Blonder diplomatically framed his proposal, the corporate strategy and planning department (CSP)—which held exclusive responsibility for corporate strategy[3]—might benefit from ODD's ambition to understand the longer-term future of technology and its implications for AT&T's business. In addition, ODD would develop tools and content for strategy making, introduce a more scientific basis to the strategy-making process, and serve as a listening post for technology developments outside AT&T. Blonder's pitch was persuasive. In February 1995, with a budget of $2 million, ODD opened for business.

The ODDsters had a higher agenda that exceeded a focus on the strategic implications of technology development. Their real mission was to challenge the status quo in order for AT&T to realize its potential as a viable competitor in the telecommunications industry. Above all, ODD hoped to accelerate the corporate recognition of what the group felt was an increasingly uncertain and challenging future by raising the quality of the strategic dialogue, by increasing the range of strategy-making tools available, and by making the strategic issues more widely and deeply felt. In ODD's view, AT&T—an incumbent exmonopolist—had become complacent. There was an urgent need to acknowledge reality. Was AT&T, with its communications technology, talent, and assets, going to direct the future of the new age of communications?

AT&T's strategy in the predivestiture years was focused on incremental growth in market share, and each year's "strategy" simply reflected the arithmetic of annual growth targets. What AT&T was doing defines the essence of a *nonstrategy*; it amounted to a linear extrapolation of the past growth curves and did not even begin to address the uncertainties around whether such growth was sustainable with AT&T's current technology position. Unfortunately, addressing even the most imminent uncertainties had no place in the AT&T strategy.

Part of this tunnel vision was attributable to the fact that strategy was the responsibility of the top executives alone. The senior management focused predominantly on regulatory issues and ignored the technology and consumer changes swirling around them. There was little strategy discussion among the lower ranks because strategy—as practiced at AT&T— seemed largely irrelevant. At the same time, the senior managers tried to convince themselves that other incumbent telcos imitating AT&T was the best compliment, and they sought comfort in strategy convergence. Unfortunately, in the world of strategy, such convergence spells bad news (or at least low profit margins).

> AT&T's strategy is sound. We know that because of the many other players in the marketplace with the same strategy.
> —Rick Miller, CFO, September 25, 1996

The ODDsters saw "that business as usual" wasn't likely to cut it in the mid-1990s. Internally, as well as externally, things were starting to get tense for AT&T: AT&T had three CEOs during the short period of 1996 to 1997 (Bob Allen, John Walter, and Mike Armstrong); there was the new Telecom Act of 1996; the Internet was growing in popularity; and there were a lot of new competitors fighting for the communications business. Time was short: The ODDsters would accelerate the corporate recognition and understanding of discontinuities—regulatory, societal, and competitive as well as technological. They would take personal risks in demonstrating to their superiors a selection of scenarios or alternative futures, some of which would be decidedly inimical to AT&T if they were to transpire. The ODDsters would refocus strategy, break orthodoxies, mobilize resources, and convert key decision makers. In so doing, like true heretics, they would remain loyal to both the corporation and their cause. ODD was a crusade and not a corporate assignment. The ODDsters could see the incredible new threats and opportunities swirling around AT&T. Could they convince some executives to see the same (and cure AT&T's opportunity deficit disorder)?

> We're in this kind of lull period where our plans are not clear because it's just messy work. One of these days we'll break out.
> —Bob Allen, in *BusinessWeek*, September 2, 1996, p. 41

As a department in the research division of Bell Labs (later the AT&T Labs), ODD occupied an organizational position that was several feet below the waterline in AT&T's corporate hierarchy. However, such a position conferred upon the nascent group a number of advantages. Foremost, and critical to its inception, ODD was in research and could therefore be safely ignored by the admirals of strategy in the CSP wheelhouse. Indeed, had ODD operated from a more potent platform, it would likely have never been sanctioned. However (and perhaps naively), ODD hoped to make up for its inferior status by generating so much intriguing content and discussion that the excitement and quality alone would compel business leaders to listen, regardless of ODD's lack of hierarchical position.

Being in a research-oriented division of AT&T Labs offered ODD other advantages besides a low profile. For example, the research division was an environment in which ODDsters could be distinctly noncorporate and even irreverent at times—requisite liberties for any group that sought to push AT&T's thinking a little further than the CSP department thought useful. Also important, research afforded ODD some space in which to think without the distractions and day-to-day turmoil that typically characterize a corporation's business units. And as members of research, ODDsters benefited from a reputation for being smart, brutally honest, and politically neutral, aloof from the intrigue, factions, and power struggles that pervade every corporation.

THE BEGINNING

Once instituted, ODD wasted no time in pursuit of its mission. A straightforward tool at hand was scenario planning that allowed the group to start talking to business units. ODD quickly found supporters among AT&T's business units for adoption of scenario planning. Early clients included the Consumer Markets Division, the Business Markets Division, and Network and Computing Services. Scenario planning provided a clever way for these business unit executives to map and begin to make sense of their considerable stress-causing anxieties. It also provided a risk-free forum to finally discuss some of the what-ifs in these "distant" scenarios. And scenario planning at its best is an engaging process; executives spent considerable time "rolling around" in the scenarios and absorbing their implications. One of the scenarios developed for the consumer services division focused on the likely outcomes of the commoditization of long-distance service, at the time in its early stages. In the scenario, long distance was positioned as an unbranded component of a larger suite of communications products or services. Seeing the AT&T brand "disappear" was of great concern to the executives.

The ODDsters of course used a variety of tools and tricks besides scenario planning. The group's goal was to make a focal issue deeply understood and deeply felt—no mere talk here. The issue was surrounded from every angle using every technique the group could find. The emergence of the Internet, naturally, was one of the main issues the group tackled. In a quest to bring corporate recognition to the transformational role of the Internet, the group's members did all the traditional things any researcher worth his or her salt would do: they constructed and publicized scenarios, did global field work to examine the emerging impact of the Internet on businesses and work, wrote white papers, and held workshops to explore question like, "What If Minutes Were Free?" (This was foresightful as no Skype yet existed.) In addition to providing expertise and "free consulting," ODD researched complex but strategically important issues as well. Moreover, it translated their significance into language that strategists could understand. For example, Internet Protocol Version 6 (IPv6) is a technical standard that defined how computers talk to each other over the Internet. A key difference between IPv6 and the existing Internet protocol was resource reservation—new circuitlike functionality that largely overcame the existing protocol's inability to support high-quality voice telephony.

ODD understood that IPv6 could have profound implications for AT&T's telephony business, which relied on a traditional circuit-switched network. But few people employed as "corporate strategists" even knew what the standard stood for. Fortunately, ODD, which combined commercial awareness and strength in technology that derived from its roots in Bell Laboratories, could demystify even the most obtuse technology and explain its business implications. Granted, it took the new Swedish intern some 20 drafts before the point got across. But persistence paid off: Anders—the intern—managed to get himself into the corporate jet with several executive vice presidents for a transcontinental journey. (Anders was one of the more daring ODDsters who had no qualms in calling an executive vice president and asking for a ride home from Seattle to New Jersey on the corporate jet.) A frantic call to the ODD headquarters immediately followed: "What should I talk to them about?" which resulted in the conviction that the executives needed to understand the significance and implications of the very protocol to begin with. So Anders gave a prep class to AT&T executives on IPv6 some 40,000 feet up.

ATTRIBUTES OF AN ODDSTER

ODDsters were, indeed, an odd group of individuals. Their backgrounds included psychology, journalism, business, chemistry, biology, physics, engineering, and materials science. Moreover, they were self-selecting. The founding group of four expanded not by overt recruitment but by attracting its own kind—like ants to sugar. Anders, for example, met up with a few ODDsters at an industry conference. After dinner and a few follow-up discussions, he was convinced that he wanted to be part of the mission. Anders then called daily, faxed articles he had written for an IT publication he founded in Sweden, sent references, and, in general, did not give up until he was hired. ODD attracted several "unofficial" members as well: AT&Ters who were "formally" employed elsewhere in the company but spent nearly all their time working on ODD projects. ODD was not the place for rapid career development; it was a mission. ODDsters' attributes were many: a willingness to ignore bureaucracy, the confidence to work without permission, and an unfailing capacity to deal with rejection. They exhibited common sense and pragmatism. They were sensitive to feedback, rabidly curious, and focused on the big picture. They were also natural and aggressive networkers.

The relationship of ODD with the AT&T establishment is noteworthy. ODDsters were not diplomats, and they certainly weren't sellouts. But nor were they suicidal. Instead, ODDsters maintained a position on the spectrum of corporate conformity that lay somewhere between diplomacy and suicide. They described themselves by the ODD word *humbitious*. That is to say, they possessed the humility to recognize that they didn't know everything, yet they were ambitious enough to be bold when their mission called for courage. Heresy is no profession for the faint of heart. To be effective, ODDsters needed extraordinary proficiency in the arts of communication, facilitation, and corporate surveillance. Communication skills were clearly necessary for articulating rational and compelling arguments across all levels of the corporation. Facilitation skills were important for managing executive-level strategy discussions. And corporate surveillance demanded an understanding of the corporate power structure, awareness of the depths and limits of managers' knowledge, and acuity to the issues that keep managers awake at night.

Some of these skills were acquired through formal training. The Global Business Network, a hub for the pragmatic intelligentsia, for example, taught a course in scenario planning and provided customized facilitation training. Other training was opportunistic. For example, ODDsters spent time shadowing representatives of the various management consulting firms from which AT&T sought strategic guidance (and bought hundreds of millions of dollars worth of advice). But for the most part, ODDster training was on the job, learning by doing. During its three-and-a-half-year life span, ODD developed a number of techniques that aspiring corporate strategists should seek to emulate. Leveraging the power of networks was perhaps the most important. The ODDsters started the Grass-Roots Network of Strategic Thinkers (GNOST) early in their existence, recognizing the need for a larger group of strategic thinkers to help complete the mission. GNOST grew to include more than 400 members, AT&Ters at all levels across the organization. GNOST connected ODD to subject experts in key areas and to key pain points in the organization in need of some ODDism. In addition, it uncovered latent heretics and activists who advanced ODD's mission in their own business units. ODD built and leveraged external networks as well, sprinkling its workshops with external perspectives and lining up speakers for its "Not Your Usual Research" series.

ODD would build networks any way it could: top down, bottom up, and sideways. It supported them with interactive tools such as a Web site and an online discussion forum, and it fed them with provocative ideas that were disseminated through workshops, social events, and thoughtful seminars.

BORROWED TIME CALLS FOR STRATEGIC IMAGINATION

In many respects, ODD was living on borrowed time, and the ODDsters knew it. When you believe passionately in your ideas and sense that time is short, you find creative ways to promote them. To this end, ODDsters developed *strategic infection points* (SIPs)—points in the organizational process at which they could introduce new strategic perspectives.

A SIP might be a neglected internal newsletter, ripe for hijacking by an undercover heretic who'd "like to help out" in its production and eventually wrest editorial control. Or a SIP might be a draft copy of an official corporate strategy document. After managing to commandeer a draft of the CSP's 1997 *AT&T Strategy and Business Planning*, ODD issued a much-revised version of the document. The "new" version got a lot more attention than any of the earlier editions had, and the CEO even requested that copies be circulated to the board.

But the best SIPs were often human rather than paper based. Indeed, ODD used a term especially for the human kind: *empty suits*. Empty suits were up-and-coming executives who needed ideas and had no problem adopting those of others. Because ODDsters cared more for the wider interest of AT&T's survival than for the narrower interest of gaining credit for their ideas, this relationship with the empty suits worked well. ODD would judge the success of its hijacking of empty suits by listening to whether its ideas (and ODD vocabulary) were making headway in the organization. A success meant that an ODD-initiated idea was claimed by an empty suit and introduced as his or her own in an executive, or even investor, meeting. A few empty suits quickly learned to ride a part of their career on the ODD idea. It was impact—not credit—ODD wanted. SIPs and empty suits are just a couple of examples of the unusual approaches and rich vocabulary conceived by ODD.

Not so long ago, a disaffected employee in one of America's largest companies caught up with me at a conference where I was speaking. In his hands was the company's glossy new performance assessment manual.... He drew my attention to the fact that only "senior executives" were to be accountable for "creating strategy." The performance criteria for "managers" and "associates" said not a word about strategy. Vibrating with indignation, he accused his employer of being uniquely stupid in having excused 99 percent of its employees from any responsibility for strategic thinking.

Surely, no other company would be so backward as to assume that only top executives could create strategy. Yes, I assured him, he had a right to be indignant. But no, his company was far from unique.

—Gary Hamel

Other nomenclature includes *data bombs, freight trains*, and *canaries*. Besides adding some fun to a difficult work environment, the code language helped ODD to establish its brand and group identity and to track the adoption of its ideas. Realizing that it was a small group with a big mission and enormous territory to conquer, ODD's distinctive approach to corporate branding quickly made it appear much larger and much more influential than it actually was. For the record, *data bombs* are statistics with disturbing implications—for example: Skype, the software application that allows the making of free voice calls over the Internet, rapidly gained tens of millions of daily users since its launch in 2003. (Its total user accounts are currently in the hundreds of millions). *Freight trains* are trends heading your way that are going to flatten you. The already happening decline in prices for long-distance telephone calls was, at the time, a freight train that was about to run over AT&T.[4] *Canaries* are scouts—people who uncover information and detect danger—in various corporate environments ranging from meeting rooms to senior executive quarters. Anders—the Swedish intern who was ODD's secret weapon—was a specialist in "being in the right places the wrong time" (that is, serendipitously gaining access to audiences and information).

THE END OF ODD (BUT THE LEGACY REMAINS)

Whereas ODD struck a chord with some executives, others viewed the group and its increasing influence with intense hostility. ODD was losing a number of its undercover supporters too, as many of its best allies left

AT&T in 1997 to 1998 in a search of better opportunities. The hostile faction directed its opprobrium primarily at Greg Blonder, who took untold arrows on behalf of the group. Eventually, Blonder's resistance wore thin. He resigned from the AT&T Labs in November 1997. ODD would survive for just eight more months without him. Of course, other factors besides Blonder's departure contributed to ODD's demise. For example, David Isenberg, one of the group's members, fell victim to an unscrupulous journalist, who gained access to internal memo he had written, "Rise of the Stupid Network," and published it in *Computer Telephony* magazine in August 1997.

The paper was Isenberg's manifesto. It ruffled a lot of feathers inside AT&T by suggesting that intelligent networks with stupid devices (such as telephones) on the periphery would soon be replaced by stupid networks with intelligent devices (such as computers) on the periphery. This tenet boded ill for AT&T, whose strategy depended on continuance of the intelligent network. "It was like a glass of cold water in the face," recalls Tom Evslin, then president of AT&T's WorldNet Service.

Opinion varies on whether Isenberg was a marked man. Certainly, his position in AT&T became uncomfortable, if not untenable, once "The Stupid Network" had leaked into the public domain. He left the company shortly thereafter. The group's position in research also became an issue. The early days, when the relative obscurity of research had afforded ODD the advantage of a low profile, had long since passed. By late 1997, ODD had become, from its opponents' perspective, all too visible. The end was nigh. It came in the fall of 1998 when AT&T Labs conducted its annual organizational review. Groups were assessed by traditional research metrics: number of patents filed, number of papers published, and so on. Corporate impact was rarely a criterion. Of course, ODD was ill placed to defend itself according to these criteria. After all, the group had been deeply involved in creating a network of strategists discussing a viable corporate strategy instead. But such a claim was viewed with disdain, given that strategy creation surely was the job the CEO and the top management were supposed to be doing. The combination of executive changes, lost supporters, and an inability to "prove" their worth in their home organization, took its toll. By July 1998, the group disbanded.

But ODD did leave an important legacy. With the group's members working tirelessly from their unsanctioned platform, they did manage to convince many of the top executives that the Internet represented a direct threat to the core value proposition of AT&T and that tinkering on a small Internet project outside of the mainstream of the business was not adequate to take care of "that Internet thing." They also painted a convincing picture of the rapid migration to an "untethered world" and accelerated AT&T's efforts into consumer wireless business.

AT&T'S STRATEGY FAILURE

So, ODD, the unwelcome messenger with rare pioneer spirit, was dead. But in the absence of an ODD-like influence, AT&T's stock price was itself showing few signs of life. Indeed, during the three-year period following ODD's disbandment and ending October 31, 2001, the stock had lost almost half its value while the Dow Jones Industrial Average had gained some 3 percent. AT&T's competitors have also performed considerably better.

When Mike Armstrong became CEO in the fall of 1997, he embarked on a bold strategy of acquiring two large cable companies (TCI and Media One) for some $100 billion. These cable interests would give AT&T, for the first time, direct access to subscribers' premises, enabling it to deliver and bundle a full line of telecommunications services (local and long-distance telephony, cable television, and high-speed Internet access) to consumers and business customers. But full integration of these services would prove more costly and more technologically complex than Armstrong had anticipated. In late 2000, in an apparent reversal of this grand integration strategy, Armstrong announced that AT&T would be split into four entities: AT&T Wireless, AT&T Broadband, AT&T Business, and AT&T Consumer.

The Origins of the Failure

Whether or not Armstrong was the "mute and deaf king" some insiders claim, AT&T's strategy-making process had unarguably been broken for some time. To understand the origins of this strategic failure, one must briefly look at AT&T's corporate history. For most of its life, which began shortly after Alexander Graham Bell's 1876 invention of the telephone, AT&T has operated in a highly regulated industry. AT&T's top-down strategy-making process worked well during those times of slow change, when its industry was regulated. The company enjoyed a measure of certainty that enabled it to plan for the needs of its customers. For example, AT&T's strategic planners could rely on the accuracy of basic demographic data to forecast long-distance call volumes or pay-phone usage.

However, such a cloistered past left AT&T unprepared for what was to follow. The 1984 breakup of the Bell System and the 1996 Telecommunications Act—the industry's most important deregulatory provisions in recent years—thrust AT&T into the midst of an industry that was replete with aggressive competitors, fast-moving technologies, and unforgiving investors. Above all, it presented uncertainty as the new constant companion to AT&T's strategists, who were accustomed to growth extrapolation based on the relatively well understood discipline of demographics. AT&T had never needed to confront the uncertainties of a dynamic and competitive market before, and it now lacked the requisite strategic skills and tools to do so. And as often seems to be the sad case, when strategy-making skills are wanting, financial deal making takes over in many a company like AT&T.

HOW TO AVOID SYSTEMIC STRATEGY FAILURE

An important key to entering a dynamic market environment from a highly regulated past is to search for the people who are the true strategists within your firm. It is unlikely the strategic minds reside in the department charged with corporate strategy in the prior, regulated world. Rather, look for people who are used to dealing with uncertainty and trained in the art of studying it. That these folks resided at the Bell Labs (and later in the AT&T Labs) should not be such a big surprise. Dealing with imperfect knowledge in an uncertain world is what scientists do.

Looking back, AT&T consistently made strategy as if the management lived alone on an island, removed from the perspectives and opinions of their own employees, not to mention the iniquities of competition and disruptive technologies. Discussion of strategic issues was suppressed in the company as a matter of policy, to protect the ignorance of top management. Any document that "could start a discussion" was not to be circulated. What company can survive when its top management uses its privileges to isolate itself in oblivion?

Furthermore, most strategy documents are empty exercises in number crunching. For example, past rounds of its *Spring Strategic Outlook* and *Fall Planning Review*—two pillars of the strategy-making process—were heavy on details such as capital expenditure budgets and earnings targets but light on consideration of the external environment—the real world in which AT&T operated. Growth by 10 percent is not a strategy—it is a number. Such is not a recipe for success. Instead, what might help is the recognition that strategy is the job of everyone inside a corporation, and good strategy can emerge from anywhere. Strategy isn't just the concern of a few executives with "strategy" buried somewhere in their titles. Pay attention: Strategic ideas may emerge from the most unlikely sources in your company—even the R&D group. The cardinal sin of management is to marginalize the smartest and most passionate people in a company due to management's own lack of enthusiasm for the future. Don't disavow the existence of ODDsters in your organization. They've probably already seen the future. And if there's a freight train heading your way, you'll be glad you hooked up with them. That way you won't end up a dead squirrel, the ODD term for a company when its strategy has failed.

P.S.: AT&T was purchased by SBC, one of the so-called baby bells, in 2005, although the combined company kept the AT&T name presumably for its consumer brand value.

SOME ODD REFLECTIONS LOOKING BACK

What ODDsters Could Have Done Differently
- Avoided the us-versus-them mentality that may have created some confrontation.
- Tuned down their slight intellectual snobbism—even if corporate strategists don't have sufficient technological background, they might have other qualities.

(continued)

- Sought to create comfort zones where those illiterate in technology and telecommunications competition could have learned without embarrassment (albeit some of this did happen through scenario planning, for instance).
- Should not have aspired to take over the strategy function of AT&T (in a clandestine manner) but sought to add value nevertheless.
- Sought to address higher audiences in top management in a more systematic manner.
- Shared their transformational experience with more people—the fervor ODD created must have scared the uninitiated within AT&T.
- Created a wider-based coalition to support their ideas (again, a lot of this did happen through the seminars, newsletters, networks).

How Management Could Have Better Taken Advantage of ODD
- Stay around longer—AT&T management changed so frequently that the new guy could never come up the learning curve fast enough.
- Have a little more courage to engage with people like the ODDsters.
- Involve the ODDsters in actual discussions about strategy—not just limit their participation to prepared input and other summary documents.
- Not make strategy by rank and file but invite those who have fresh perspectives and some new ideas.
- Look beyond the usual suspects and consultants when engaging people in strategy discussions.
- Go to the company cafeteria to see what's going on. As one of the ODDsters—who had gained some fame in the firm as a strategist—noted: "When I entered the company cafeteria, I felt like one of the Beatles—everyone wanted to rally around and talk to me."

When ODDsters Become Particularly Important to Your Firm—and When You Need to Start Paying Attention to Them
- There is a lot of discontinuous change, and perhaps a move from regulated to deregulated (or reregulated) environments. Look for ODDsters for new competitive perspectives.

- There are big leadership changes in the company. There is a lot of politics and positioning for the top jobs. Look for ODDsters for unbiased opinions, industry know-how, and future visions.
- There is a growing gap between the technology presently in use and the technology that is replacing the one in use. Look for ODDsters to have a point of view.
- There is a lot of uncertainty about standards, competitive dominance, and newcomers' roles. Look for ODDsters to assess what's really going on.
- The quality of existing strategy discussion in the firm is low. Look for ODDsters to add some ideas and color.
- The morale is low, and hope is needed in the form of a new vision, new strategy, new energy. Look for ODDsters to add some vibrancy.

How to Find an ODDster When You Need One
- Listen to the most intriguing strategy discussion in the firm, anywhere, any time. Join it.
- Look for the most thought-provoking article in the company newsletter. Go talk to the author.
- Invite people to write a competing strategy document to the official one. Promise the authors that they can stay anonymous if they so wish. Read the competing strategy documents and promote the winner to a strategy officer (if the person chooses to reveal his or her identity, of course).
- Go to the cafeteria and listen to what and whom people talk about.
- Ask five different people who do not know each other in the firm who they think is the best strategic mind the firm has outside the strategy department. Go talk to the people they name and ask, again, who they think are the best strategists. And so on.
- Look for people who have the most connections to the rest of the world outside the firm.
- Talk to your customers, your partner companies, and your competitors. Who do they think has strategic insight in your company?

STEP 3.
REHEARSING
A CULTURE OF
RESILIENCE

The basic thesis of this book is that our organizations will be required to show resilience of a much greater degree than before to make it to the future. The five ways described in Part Three to building resilience are a start. Once resilience is built into the organization, it needs to be rehearsed. How?

The prior case studies have given some indications as to how to rehearse resilience. The leading U.S. consumer electronics retailer experimented on management practices to overcome impediments to change. The Afghan students rehearse resilience partly as a way of life due to harsh conditions but also as a determined aspiration to become entrepreneurs. Resource scarcity requires resilience but also constant innovation to overcome daily challenges. Resilient thinking can be exercised in a playful exercise, as did the ODDsters at AT&T, seeking to engage business units in a totally different kind of future strategy conversation and developing an entirely new strategy vocabulary as part of the game. (Chapter 13, "Postcard No. 3 from San Jose, California: Tempered Radicalism and Management Practices That Stick," will expand on the success factors of such organizational activism in this section.)

There are, in addition to the resilience building blocks described in the previous chapters, a number of growing phenomena with the potential to help. They are ways of unleashing human capability for solving problems and joining forces between unlikely partners and across the globe. Engagement, passion for innovation, crowdsourcing, institutional activism, and inventive experimentation are departures from the standard organizational tool kit of hierarchical control, task specialization, process standardization, or reward-oriented performance control. User-driven innovation, positive psychology, and open innovation promise further progress. They certainly suggest that we need to refresh our management approaches in building a culture of resilience.

SOME STRATEGIES FOR UNLEASHING HUMAN POTENTIAL

- *Engagement and passion for innovation:* Focus on the potential contribution the work can make, not its technical execution, as a managerial challenge (see Chapter 11, "Postcard No. 1 from the Silicon Valley, California: For the Love of It!—The Resilience of Amateurs").
- *Crowdsourcing:* Bring the masses to contribute through social media and open organizing (see Chapter 12, "Postcard No. 2 from Hanover, New Hampshire: 'We Want Our Country Back!'—The Emergence and Resilience of Open Organizing").
- *Institutional activism:* How to develop politically smart strategies for change no matter where you are in the organizational hierarchy (see Chapter 13, "Postcard No. 3 from San Jose, California: Tempered Radicalism and Management Practices That Stick").
- *Inventive experimentation:* A passionate call for developing management innovations jointly with scholars and practitioners through inventive experimentation (see Chapter 14, "Postcard No. 4 from Woodside, California: The Challenge of Inventive Experimentation to Management Research—Or, Who Is Responsible for Developing New Management Practice?").

Still other promising strategies may include these:

- *User-driven innovation:* Search for already-existing solutions invented by lead users who are closest to the inventive need.
- *Positive psychology:* Make use of low-cost ways to increase people's motivation (focus on life-giving forces rather than shortcomings or illnesses).
- *Open innovation:* Source innovative ideas and solutions from anywhere in the world (similar to crowdsourcing).

Think of the four stories that follow as postcards from the resilience edge. They are hopefully provocative but also tempered. They tell tales of different aspects of resilience—of love, of rise to the challenge, of communities, of countries, of experimentation, and of institutions. The first postcard is about the amateur in us.

POSTCARD NO. 1 FROM THE SILICON VALLEY, CALIFORNIA: FOR THE LOVE OF IT!— THE RESILIENCE OF AMATEURS

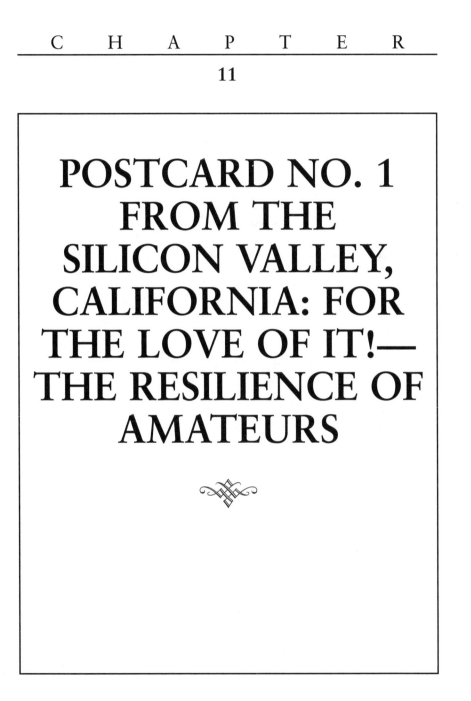

Would-be innovators in large corporations are sometimes offered the following advice: "Behave as if you were independently wealthy!" The key resilience word is "independently." With independence, would-be innovators can make their own judgments without relying on managerial permission or control. Independence confers a privilege on those with a passion for creativity and experimentation—the opportunity to follow one's instinct without being under some externally imposed obligation. Is such an approach feasible or advantageous in a corporate setting?

Apparently not, based on how few corporations pursue this approach. Despite 3M's lauded and well-published rule of allowing its researchers 15 percent discretionary time, only a few other companies (see the sidebar) have adopted this or a similar best practice.

THE INDEPENDENCE FORMULA

Google is one of the few firms that sees exceptional value in the independent innovator. The company has a management philosophy that requires it to dedicate 10 percent of its investment to employee-initiated projects unrelated to the core business. Google calls this the "70-20-10 formula." According to the CEO Eric Schmidt, 70 percent of the company's resources are channeled to the core business of Internet search and advertising, 20 percent are channeled to adjacent products such as desktop and product search services. The remaining 10 percent are focused on highly experimental products—innovations important for the long term.

This chapter is adapted from Liisa Välikangas and Quintus Jett, "The Golden Spur: Innovation Independence." Reprinted from *Strategy & Leadership*, vol. 34, no. 5, 2006, pp. 41–45, with permission from the Emerald Group.

WHY INDEPENDENCE MATTERS[1]

Most companies don't encourage their employees to pursue innovation. Despite the belief that we toil in an age when "knowledge workers" are key to the success of institutions, few companies grant their workforces the independence that their capabilities would seem to merit. Would it be so radical for firms to create a market for innovation and strategy ideas? Could any employee suggest a promising beginning of an idea that others could build on? Such markets for ideas are currently being experimented on; yet they still face hurdles in requiring that employees have the capacity and permission to volunteer part of their time to work on the ideas they feel passionate about.

Today's reward systems pose a further roadblock in corporations to such new thinking. As Amabile (1993) has found, monetary compensation shifts the motivational basis of behavior from internal to external rewards. Once financial rewards become the principal incentive, we shift our behavior— and sometimes our beliefs—to justify our reward-seeking activities. We perform because we get paid, not because the work has its own intrinsic value. Such extrinsically motivated behavior tempts us to give up some of our integrity. (Hence the recent financial crisis during which a number of parties can be said to have compromised their independent judgment.) In accepting the predominance of extrinsic rewards over intrinsic motivation, we give up some independence of belief and purpose (and potentially also our integrity). Our work loses its personal relevance, and we significantly reduce our joy in creativity. We submit to doing what we get paid for.

There is a minor yet highly visible rebellion going on, however. Those who call themselves "hackers" are experimenting on a lifestyle unencumbered by corporate "corruption." A student in Helsinki wrote Linux, the open source operating system, with help from 120,000 friends all around the world, for free (Tuomi, 2003). Some have testified to the morality of the hacker ethic and to the preeminence of a hacker society. Manifestos have been written; fierce independence is celebrated, and fun has been elevated as the über-motivation to rule. But this is too nouveau age: we do not all wish or need to become hackers to be free. In fact, computer enthusiasts have simply discovered a very old truth. When you do something for the love (or fun) of it, it elevates your being and frees your spirit. There are echoes in this way of working that suggest true satisfaction. At our best, or at our most human, we are all like amateurs when we work, or increasingly, dedicated idealists who work toward a cause, skillfully harnessing global networks for change.

THE EXAMPLE OF AMATEURS

Idealistic amateurs are nothing new of course. Jenny Uglow's *The Lunar Men* tells a story of a group of amateur inventors, scientists, and manufacturers paving the way for the Industrial Revolution in the eighteenth and nineteenth centuries. Most were nonconformists and freethinkers, who pursued scientific questions out of curiosity. Albert Einstein engaged in science in addition to his duties as a patent office clerk. Samuel Morse, the inventor of the Morse code, was a book publisher and a famed portrait painter. More recently, amateur activity was manifest in the Homebrew Computer Club, which spawned Steve Jobs's and Steve Wozniak's ideas for a personal computer in the 1970s. To quote its convener Gordon French, the club was "the damned finest collection of engineers and technicians that you could possibly get under one roof." (The roof was French's garage during the inaugural meeting on March 5, 1975.)

The word *amateur* is a complex one. By one meaning, it indicates limited skill and amateurishness, as opposed to professionalism. Yet its older meaning comes (via French) from the Latin word *love* (*l'amour*). Thus the word can mean doing something for the love of it, as a pastime perhaps, but with dedication. Amateurs engage in activities they are passionate about. Amateurs today—whether computer programmers contributing to open source projects or the grassroots volunteers contributing to political campaigns—are predominantly well educated and very informed, and they have professional skills. The "amateur" virtuosi have proven themselves capable or exceptional in their professional fields and now wish to apply their skills to causes they care about in new fields. Indeed, the capabilities of professionals and amateurs can overlap significantly (Önkal, Yates, Simga-Mugan, & Öztin, 2003).

SET THEM FREE

Nonetheless, many of us persist in our belief that the best-performing, most complex organizations are those inhabited and managed by professionals. We see in Max Weber's concept of bureaucracy the significance of professional specialization. The idealization was an attempt to make organizations more accountable, capable, and reliable. As such, the commitment to professionalization was highly successful in increasing production efficiency and reliability. Yet at the same time, we lost some of the freedom to explore that came with amateurism.

Allow me be provocative to make this point. The Industrial Revolution may have made us rich but it also subjugated us. This servitude is of a subtle kind: we get paid for doing what we are told to do. Now you may argue that—as a superb knowledge worker—you really enjoy your work. So do I. You may indeed love your window office or even find your cubicle more bearable than cartoonist Scott Adams did. But in accepting this low standard, we have all missed the point. Fool yourself all you want by evoking the pleasure of paid work—your psyche will tell you that you, or at least the part of you that is at work, has been bought. This may be why so many people check that which is the best of themselves at the door when they come to work.

In the competition with the work drudge, we believe that amateurs are making a comeback. The amateur rebellion is constituted on the strongest grounds—personal beliefs, aspirations, and intrinsic motivations—all that is best about us as human beings. Amateurs, in Freeman Dyson's words, are a measure of the freedom of a society: "In almost all the varied walks of life, amateurs have more freedom to experiment and innovate" (Dyson, 2002). Amateurs are not under pressure for short-term performance or strict job descriptions or titles, nor are they under managerial surveillance. Amateurs have the independence to innovate. They may take time to learn and move from field to field, finding creativity in the convergence of technology and the combinatorial possibilities found when crossing different industries and professional specialties (Johansson, 2004). There is indeed value in being a dilettante. Rather than being bound by professional conventions that might be outdated and no longer productive, amateurs have freedom—to experiment and openly explore a wide array of fringe options.

This rebellion for amateur freedom is facilitated by communications technologies that enable people to participate increasingly on their own terms. Such technological progress may aid the eventual arrival of an "individualized corporation" (Bartlett & Ghoshal, 1999). Such organizational visions echo notions of democracy—a governance system that is premised on the conviction that each person is the best judge of that person's needs (and desires to contribute) and that this judgment should be protected from manipulation (March & Olsen, 1995).

This liberating shift may well give companies what is necessary to unleash their human talent and raise the level of innovation needed to compete with cheap (yet increasingly skilled) labor in emerging economies such as China and India. To accomplish this feat, however, there are many challenges managers will need to embrace to unleash innovation. To start, managers must respect their employees' independence—the very source of innovation. The case for innovation is the case for the labor of love—that is, the work of amateurs.

BUT HOW?

Here are two concrete examples of amateur organization. At a leading nationwide retailer (the story told in greater length in Chapter 9), a group of people formed an initiative to create a marketplace of ideas and talent. The idea was deceptively simple: Anyone could pitch a project and invite others to join it. The hypothesis was that such an avenue for ideas and commitment would increase productivity and address an endemic scarcity of resources. ("No, we don't have anyone with free time at the moment to assign to the project.") The experiment's successes confirmed that many people will indeed welcome an avenue for amateuring. Even more importantly, the marketplace for ideas and talent might provide a strategy for a much smoother resource allocation than the current corporate HR processes offered. Rather than a manager's allocating staff to projects, employees contributed to projects they judged most compelling. For a company that employed more than 100,000 people, such talent and time fluidity would be a critical source of competitive advantage. For the marketplace to become a success, however, three conditions had to be maintained:

1. Any employee could join any project of his or her choosing part-time.
2. Any project that attracted more than three volunteer-amateurs would have legitimacy and, thus, the right to proceed initially (although it could later be combined with another project).
3. Project members were asked to keep a record of discovered ideas that simultaneously held promise for themselves, personally, and for the company. This information could then be gathered across projects and analyzed strategically for emergent patterns.

Thus, there is value to a marketplace beyond the individual projects—it is a source of strategic insight externally, on the wider business environment, as well as internally, on workforce interests and capabilities. (How many managers actually know what really motivates their employees beyond adding money to the paycheck? How many managers know of the passions of their employees, if not listed on a résumé and not otherwise made visible by their immediate responsibilities?)

Another example of amateur activity comes from a very different domain of activity. The Dean for America (DFA) presidential campaign mobilized large numbers of volunteer-activists who were committed to bringing change to the political landscape in the United States (see Postcard No. 2 in the next chapter). The Dean for America campaign functioned simultaneously as an organization and as a broader community that encompassed numerous geographically dispersed amateurs, many of whom were operating outside the direct control of the campaign. The campaign broke Democratic Party fund-raising records by employing innovative ways of harnessing small contributions, including a "thermometer" concept, one popularized by the United Way. The Dean campaign's staff members adapted this concept by posting online a graphic of a baseball bat and player, where the bat served as the marker that indicated fund-raising progress. As a way of further supporting the fund-raising bat, the Dean campaign's software programmers created an application that enabled the community activists to create their own "personal bat" Web pages. These pages provided the individuals who signed up with their own digital fund-raising center. They could set their own fund-raising goals, customize their own fund-raising appeals, and manage their own e-mail contact lists to make solicitations for money on behalf of the campaign. The money they raised fed directly to the Dean campaign. Thus the amateur community was able to significantly contribute to the fund-raising activities of the campaign, building early credibility through strong financial results when the campaign was still considered one without any real credibility (see, for example, the *Economist*, "Cut from the Same Cloth," November 29, 2003).

ARE WE ALL AMATEURS NOW?

Amateurism taps our inner strength by inviting us to show what we really care about: putting our efforts where our passions lie. Not all of these efforts bear fruit or are competitive (we all are familiar with someone who really likes to help but cannot). Also, amateurism is no panacea; instead, it is like time management, servant leadership, and other managerial approaches that are generally useful but not the absolute or final cures for complex problems in organizations.

Amateurism is most suited for task environments that require taking risks and making discoveries. Organizations must be reliable and committed to routine, but these same qualities destroy innovativeness. While the intent, and often the effect, of bureaucratic controls is to add to reliability, the same measures reduce the autonomy of employees and volunteers and also the free reign to make choices when personal initiative and inner commitment are most desired.

In this age when professionalism is so dominant, amateur creativity and effort bring forth new ideas, as well as playful energy that animates organizational routines. Today's leadership challenge for resilience is learning to manage the independent thinkers who emerge within this new amateurism.

POSTCARD NO. 2 FROM HANOVER, NEW HAMPSHIRE: "WE WANT OUR COUNTRY BACK!"— THE EMERGENCE AND RESILIENCE OF OPEN ORGANIZING

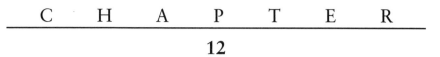

This next postcard, written with Quintus Jett (of Dartmouth College[1]), is about a pioneering political campaign that had some aspects that were highly resilient, others not so.

DEAN FOR AMERICA

The Dean for America campaign was the precursor to the sophisticated use of the Internet in presidential campaigning: it was the trailblazer that President Obama successfully employed in 2008.

Dean for America (DFA), Howard Dean's campaign to become U.S. president in 2004, is widely known for using Internet technology to fundraise, engage its supporters, and mobilize grassroots volunteers. It grew quickly and unexpectedly throughout 2003. It raised unprecedented amounts of money for a political campaign that relied primarily on small donations of $100 or less. It had numerous supporters who created and ran unofficial groups and volunteer organizations throughout the United States, as well as abroad. Overall, the campaign's use of the Internet as an organizing tool helped elevate Howard Dean from a long-shot presidential candidate to the frontrunner within his political party. According to a large random sample survey of Dean's supporters and activists (Pew Research, 2005), Dean for America reached many people who had not previously

This chapter is modified from an article by Quintus Jett and Liisa Välikangas titled "Toward Open-Sourced Design: Digital Media and the Potential for Organizations to Evolve," presented at the Academy of Management, New Orleans, 2006. See also Quintus Jett and Liisa Välikangas. "The Gamble of Open Organizing." Dartmouth College, Center for Digital Strategies, Working Paper, Series 04-1, Winter 2004.

been politically active beyond voting. The survey, which used the Dean campaign's own e-mail list of supporters, indicated that most Dean activists were middle-aged, contrary to many popular perceptions, and that they remained engaged in political action many months after Howard Dean suspended his presidential campaign, volunteering and donating money to support the eventual party nominee John Kerry.

THE SETTING

In the United States, a presidential campaign organization must grow significantly during the two years preceding the general election. First, to have electoral impact, a campaign needs to grow from inception to a multi-million-dollar organization within 12 months, before the primary season starts (Appleman, 2004). Therefore, in its early stages, the primary activities of a presidential campaign are fund-raising and contacting the potential voters in a variety of states and constituencies. Next, after the primary season, if and when candidates win the nomination of their political party, their campaign organizations must further develop and grow, in preparation for the general election. Otherwise, if candidates lose their bid for party nomination, their campaign organizations are terminated since the purpose of electing the candidate has gone unfulfilled.

Howard Dean's U.S. presidential campaign is distinguished from the evolution of most other campaigns in two ways. First, it evolved from a negligible to a dominant force in the primary race unexpectedly, during the 12 months preceding the start of the 2004 presidential primary season. Dean had been governor of Vermont, a predominantly rural state that has one of the lowest populations in the United States and has far fewer residents than many major U.S. cities. Although he was not taken seriously as a presidential candidate in early 2003 (see, for example, the *Economist*, "Cut from the Same Cloth," November 29, 2003), he was by early 2004 the frontrunner who overshadowed all other Democratic Party candidates in national press coverage, money, and crowds (Littwin, 2004). However, the end of Dean's campaign was as unexpected and dramatic as its rise. Dean lost every state election once the primaries started, beginning with the caucuses in the state of Iowa, before he suspended his campaign. His only electoral victory came a few weeks later after his campaign had ended, when he won the primary in his home state of Vermont.

A second distinguishing, more resilient feature in the evolution of Dean's campaign was that many organized activities of its supporters persisted well past the campaign's end. When Howard Dean ended his presidential bid, he expressed an intention to launch a new organization that would offer continuity to the supporters who participated in his campaign. Within months, he had founded Democracy for America, relying on the remaining list of supporters from his campaign. The purpose of the new organization was to encourage ordinary citizens to run for elected office, while endorsing and supporting candidates who were "socially progressive and fiscally responsible."

Meanwhile, a number of Dean's supporters persisted in volunteering within the grassroots organizations that they had founded or participated in during the campaign. By 2005, one year after exiting the presidential race, Howard Dean was elected chairman of his party. His new organization had grown its list of supporters to approximately 600,000 people, the level seen at the peak of his presidential campaign in January 2004. Also, a number of organizations founded by the campaign's grassroots volunteers had started formulating and executing their own initiatives, maintaining various degrees of contact with Democracy for America and operating independently. For instance, two state-based organizations founded by Dean volunteers—California for Democracy and Democracy for Texas— each had participant lists of tens of thousands of people, had developed its own governance, and had designed political actions within its state that were independent of Democracy for America's plans and initiatives. Many additional grassroots groups from Dean's campaign were acting similarly, in various degrees and at different levels of scale.

THE DEAN FOR AMERICA CAMPAIGN: ORIGINS AND GROWTH

My coauthor Quintus Jett and I studied the design and evolution of Howard Dean's presidential campaign from two perspectives: the capacity of the campaign goals to accommodate a lot of different political aspirations (as in, "We want out country back") and the capacity of the evolving campaign organization to attract large numbers of contributors. We believe that these two aspects have implications beyond political campaigning to resilient organizing.

"We Want Our Country Back"

On March 15, 2003, at the state of California's Democratic convention, Dean, a presidential hopeful and a medical doctor from the small state of Vermont, introduced himself as representing "the Democratic wing of the Democratic Party." His comment was linked to his vocal opposition to the Iraq war, which was to begin a few days later. The remarks drew an enthusiastic reception, similar to what Dean received when he first gave his remarks at the February meeting in Washington, DC. In addition, toward the end of his remarks, Dean said: "I want my country back!"

In his book that reflects on his experience as a presidential candidate, Dean reflects on that formative day saying that "the words just rose from my gut." He describes being struck by the emotional reaction of the audience as he further declared, "We want our country back!" (Dean & Warner, 2004: 1). The theme became one of the informal rallying calls of the campaign, used regularly by Howard Dean in his speeches and adopted in the public dialogue and expressions of some of Dean's supporters. "Taking the country back" became a shorthand phrase for a variety of general aspirations that campaign participants shared: standing up to Christian evangelists within the Republican Party; helping the Democratic Party rediscover and fight for its principles; restoring hope in the country's democracy; regaining respect for America around the world; and envisioning the inclusion of all people in America's public life, irrespective of their gender, race, or sexual orientation. The theme soon became an encompassing and engaging goal, adopted and varied by his followers.

The Evolution of Fund-Raising Activities

Beyond an enticing goal, a candidate needs money. After filing to run for president in mid-2002, Dean was lacking in fund-raising prospects. In January 2003, the *Economist* magazine concluded that Dean looked like a typical candidate who had no hope of being a contender but who nevertheless had interesting ideas and a record in the area of health-care reform. Nevertheless, as the year 2003 progressed, Dean was to raise more money than any other presidential candidate in his party. After lagging in fund-raising in early 2003, compared to the candidates who were widely perceived as major candidates, Dean's campaign raised the most money of any Democratic candidate during the second quarter. By the end of the third quarter, Dean for America's cumulative fund-raising for the year had surpassed the other campaigns, and it had broken his party's fund-raising record for a single quarter by a presidential candidate, which was previously set by Bill Clinton as an incumbent president during his 1996 reelection campaign. Howard Dean completed the calendar year with $50 million in total fund-raising, a level far enough above the other candidates to help grant a perception that he would be his party's eventual candidate for president.

Small Donations via the Internet

"Small donations" soon became a focus of the Dean campaign. To qualify as the first Democratic candidate for federal matching funds for the 2004 presidential elections would mean raising a minimum of $5,000 in multiple states. Although other political campaign organizations have used the Internet for fund-raising (for example, presidential candidate John McCain did so in the 2000 primaries), it was in March 2003 that the Dean campaign began to rely on and solicit small donations via the Internet as a public operational strategy. In an inaugural post on the campaign's Call to Action Blog on March 15, DFA campaign manager Joe Trippi invited supporters to contribute whatever they could in advance of March 30, the important deadline to report fund-raising for the first quarter of 2003 to the Federal Elections Commission.

Dean's campaign departed from this reporting practice by making its fund-raising status public during the final days of the second quarter in 2003. The campaign used a fund-raising "thermometer" concept, one popularized by the United Way in which the fund-raising organization has a graphical representation of its goal and indicates with a rising red marker the cumulative progress toward that goal. The Dean campaign's staff members adapted this concept by posting online a graphic of a baseball bat and player, where the bat served as the marker that indicated fund-raising progress. The campaign raised $3 million in the last nine days of June, well over a half-million dollars on the last day of the quarter. Its receipts for the quarter totaled over $7.5 million, surpassing an initial public goal of approximately $6 million, and the campaign raised more money for the quarter than any of the other competing campaigns.

Internet-enabled tactics such as the fund-raising bat and associated personal bat pages available to supporters helped Dean's campaign set new fund-raising records for a Democratic presidential candidate, both for a single quarter and for the entire year before the presidential primaries. These tactics entailed using digital media applications to report fund-raising progress both regularly and publicly, to make the donation process convenient and interactive, and to help supporters solicit their personal networks for additional contributions.

The Evolution of Voter Contact Activities

Howard Dean's list of supporters at the start of 2003 was hundreds of people, a list too small to build a national campaign organization (Trippi, 2004), but it was to expand significantly by the end of 2003, enough to include numerous unofficial groups located in many different places. Dean's campaign organization performed a number of activities to facilitate contact with its potential supporters and voters: developing a business relationship with the Internet start-up Meetup.com, a service that used online tools to help people with common interests find each other offline in their local communities; developing its official Web site Blog for America as a virtual campaign headquarters; and developing online software to facilitate individuals' finding local campaign events.

Dean for America also facilitated contact among campaign participants through its GetLocal tools, which its software programmers developed and made available for the campaign Web site's visitors to post, locate, and sign up for DFA events. A recurring theme in DFA's use of online tools for making contact with potential voters was translating online behavior into offline action. Meetup.com and GetLocal tools were online services that facilitated in-person contact. The campaign's blog served as an online channel to making calls to action. Some actions could be performed online—for example, registering with Meetup.com or sharing news about the campaign via e-mail. Other actions—for instance, writing letters to undecided voters in early primary states—were offline activities that the campaign used online tools to facilitate (that is, making the addresses of the undecided voters available for download from the campaign's Web site).

Although the official campaign organization initiated contact between itself and its supporters (and created means of contact among supporters), there were still plenty of kinds of cross-communication that were beyond the campaign's planning, expectations, and control. Months before Dean's campaign launched its official blog, there were already people who had taken an interest in Howard Dean's candidacy and who were expressing that interest through online community forums. For example, Dean Nation was a blog that was launched in 2002, about six months before the start of the official campaign's blog.

There was a lot of informality and openness in all communications. Although Blog for America was an official campaign space, its comments area functioned as a public square. Visitors were not required to register until many months later in January 2004. In 2003, the blog was open to any-one to comment anonymously, including visitors who opposed Dean's can-didacy. Also, every official post by the campaign was normally treated by visitors as an "open thread"—whatever was the official post topic, visitor comments generally went off topic very rapidly. However, even when they were off topic, many of the comments and much of the dialogue and the exchange of information and Web links were related in some form to Howard Dean and his campaign, or more broadly to politics. The Blog for America comments space developed a community atmosphere as regular visitors learned to recognize each other. It also became a place where visitors gave their immediate reactions to the campaign's events and circumstances.

The campaign's blog comments grew throughout 2003 to hundreds per posted topic and to thousands per day. Furthermore, the comment area regu-larly provided a window into the shared points of view and the debates among Dean's supporters, as well as their debates against Dean's detractors who would visit. The Blog for America comment space, overall, made the commu-nications, reactions, and spirit of Dean's supporters visible and transparent.

In addition to Blog for America, cross-communication among Dean's supporters took place through numerous kinds of unofficial DFA groups and organizations that formed throughout the year 2003. Many were local, as an outgrowth of Dean Meetup events. Others were regional or state based, like those in California, Texas, Massachusetts, Georgia, or Kansas and Missouri. Most of these unofficial groups were in states that did not have official DFA field organizations because the states were not immediately relevant or critical in the early stages of the 2004 primary voting. Some volunteers from these groups, in addition to participating in their local meeting and visibility events, would travel to where they could be most useful to the campaign; for instance, a number of Massachusetts-based volunteers reported that they had traveled to the competitively significant neighboring state of New Hampshire. As unofficial DFA groups formed, they provided another means for new and existing volunteers to follow and remain in touch with the campaign's developments, through forms and channels different from the official campaign messages. Other than an alphabetical roll call of unofficial DFA groups on the sidebar of the Blog for America Web site, the official campaign imposed no governance or cross-channels of communications for these groups.

HOW TO LOSE AN ELECTION

The campaign began its collapse in January 2004. Howard Dean was at the time the dominant frontrunner and seen as the almost inevitable party nominee, but he lost the first primary in Iowa. Following the loss, his impassioned speech in Iowa at a rally of his volunteers was widely broadcast on mass media outlets and frequently replayed and lampooned. A week later, Dean lost the primary in New Hampshire, a state that borders his home state of Vermont. The campaign full of surprises had come to an abrupt end.

GRASSROOTS PROJECTS FOLLOWING THE START OF THE OFFICIAL CAMPAIGN'S COLLAPSE: THE *HOW IT REALLY HAPPENED* VIDEO

The evening that Howard Dean came in third in the Iowa caucuses, he came to a large rally of his supporters, most of whom were out-of-state volunteers who had traveled to Iowa to help the campaign in the final week before the voting. His impassioned speech to these supporters was widely broadcast, replayed, and lampooned. It was singled out overnight as the moment that he lost all credible chance of winning his party's nomination.

One of Dean's supporters in the audience, however, was a documentary film maker, and he recognized problems with the speech that was broadcast. The camera angle on Dean did not show the large, excited crowd surrounding the stage, missing the context of Dean's remarks (which is why the film maker chose to shoot his own footage during the speech from within the crowd). The broadcast of Dean's speech also muted the stomping and cheering of the crowd. As it was discovered later, it was due to a directional microphone that captured Dean raised voice to be heard above the crowd but without the crowd's loud background noise (and their visible excitement) to show why he was so loud and animated. The film maker quickly attempted to get his video public because it showed the Dean's speech from the audience's perspective: excited crowds that were cheering so loudly that the infamous broadcasted "scream" that Dean made was barely audible. The film maker says that many Dean supporters tried to help him get the video to the DFA campaign organization. Despite their efforts, there was no response.

So the film maker put the video on his Web site for viewing. A link to the site was shared repeatedly by Dean supporters in the Blog for America comments space, and news spread of it. The grassroots-run Dean Rapid Response Network (another informal organization) put a link to the video on its Web site home page. Much traffic flooded the documentary film maker's Web site. He began to get calls of complaint from his Internet service provider, and he concluded that he would have to remove the video from his site. His service charges were determined by the bandwidth that his Web site used, and the traffic to view the video was so high that he expected to owe $20,000 in several days, by the end of the week.

Someone suggested that he set up a PayPal account, a service that facilitates the electronic transfer of funds using an existing credit card or checking account. He set up the account, receiving sufficient money

(*continued*)

from visitors to keep the video active on the site, and several Dean supporters also agreed to host the video on their own Web sites as a means of sharing the high-volume traffic. The next week, the video was played by *ABC News* as an account of "what really happened" the night of Dean's infamous scream. Despite the news interest, the official campaign apparently made the decision not to respond, based on the view that any response would keep the original incident in the news. Or perhaps the campaign, by then, had lost its determination to fight.

OBSERVATIONS ON ORGANIZING AND DIGITAL MEDIA

What can be learned from the Dean campaign that is relevant beyond political organizing?

First, digital media are making the creation and sustenance of special-purpose organizations more affordable. Prior to the mainstream convergence of computing and communications technologies (that is, with the popularization of the Internet in 1993 and 1994), there was a claim that people with few institutional resources should not start organizations as they cannot sustain them and that these organizations would therefore become exploited by existing organizations that are powerful and resourceful (Piven & Cloward, 1979; Conell & Voss, 1990). Today, we see digital media facilitating the emergence of low-cost organizations that are created to serve social movements or special interests on their own terms. Digital media technologies are known to reduce the communication and coordination costs of organizations, as the associated tools and infrastructure themselves become more pervasive and affordable (for example, Malone, 2004). In addition, digital media further empowers individuals and small groups to create (digitally enabled) organizations that are capable of reaching nonlocal sources of support to ensure critical size.

Second, serendipity (or luck) plays a role. In many respects, the Dean campaign fortuitously benefited from digital technologies that were publicly available and *preadaptive* (that is, they could be crafted or customized with little cost). Available digital media technologies (blogging software) facilitated the creation of Howard Dean interest groups that would be reasonably sustainable. The campaign organization quickly adopted a different set of digital media tools from Meetup.com to establish a physical presence in many local communities. It then adapted an existing concept (the fund-raising thermometer) to a digital media form, using it to collect the financial resources needed to remain competitive and then dominate the fund-raising of competitors. The campaign organization's use of these digital tools became a natural aspect of its fund-raising and voter contact activities, which may have encouraged the growing community of Dean's supporters to seek adoption and use of similar tools, in order to create and sustain their unofficial DFA groups.

When the campaign organization was suspended, due to its failure to win primaries and depletion of money, its groups and communities of supporters remained, having been created and (in part) sustained through their use of digital media technologies. The resilience of these communities provided the resources for Howard Dean to retire his campaign debts, as well as to create and sustain a new organization Democracy for America, which coexisted with a number of prior unofficial groups from Dean's campaign that have since become legal organizations.

The third, and increasingly commonplace, observation is that digital media tools help make special-purpose organizations and communities most visible to those who want to find them. Many digital applications were developed by the campaign; yet without the availability of Yahoo! groups, Meetup.com, and blogging capabilities, in particular, the DFA would have been severely handicapped in its capacity to reach a wide community of supporters. These tools added a veneer of publicity to discourses and events that until then might have been only locally known and observed. Thus, with the use of digital media tools and infrastructure (for example, online search engines), people are increasingly in the position to attract and search for others who share their interests but who are beyond the boundaries of what is geographically or socially approachable (Cattani, Pennings, & Wezel, 2003).

Once these special-purpose organizations and communities are discovered online, further communication and actions can subsequently occur in other venues (for example, via in-person meetings and telephone) in a mix of virtual and physical, online and offline activities. After discovery, these organizations or communities might employ strategies that bind transient visitors to their cause for an enduring way, for instance, by using calls for action that are personally relevant, invoking meaningful imagery and symbols (such as the baseball bat) as community rituals, and inviting small tangible acts and contributions that help cultivate larger commitments in the future. Thus, the visibility of online activities may provide an initial step toward capturing regular visitors, who can help sustain an organization or community.

EVOLVABILITY AND OPEN-COMMUNITIES ORGANIZING

In a qualitative study, Rindova and Kotha (2001) focused on the executive team's ability to "morph" its organization (that is, to design it to be evolvable). "Make no deal that limits Yahoo!'s future evolvability." However, in the Dean campaign, such evolvability—the managerial intent of being careful with actions that might close out future options—does not reflect the actions that contributed to the Dean campaign's unexpected growth. Instead, the campaign organization's growth was derived from its connections to the potential outside in the larger civic community. The Dean for America campaign achieved unexpected growth and significance by blurring the boundaries between who is "in" and who is "out." Independent volunteers and unofficial groups were embraced as full participants, perhaps even owners, of the campaign, despite being outside the campaign organization and therefore beyond its prescribed roles of who must do what.

Such roles for nonpaid participants, outside traditional managerial control, are becoming increasingly important in "open" organizations that range in purpose from political campaigns to software development to scientific research. To some extent such amateur activity (also discussed in Chapter 11, "Postcard No. 1: For the Love of It!—The Resilience of Amateurs") has always been manifest in free societies, but the role of digital technology may be coordinating such activity to an extent never feasible before. Yet the tapping of the communities outside of organizations for volunteers is not new: the *Oxford English Dictionary* project in the nineteenth century used hundreds of volunteers from a variety of physical locations (and social positions) in a decades-long effort to correct deficiencies in existing dictionaries (Winchester, 1998, 2003).

IMPLICATIONS FOR RESILIENT ORGANIZING

The Dean campaign contains important ideas as to how organizational designers can make their organizations more like an evolutionary playground and less like an ideal form, a master designer's one shot at an efficient, intelligent design. More by camping in a tent than living in a palace [a famous phrase used by Hedberg, Nystrom, and Starbuck (1976) to convey the promise of self-organizing], Dean for America transformed from being an insignificant campaign to a formidable one (before its coming to an end, as most campaigns do). Yet this evolution was not a foresight that Howard Dean possessed as a stretched goal or aspiration early in the campaign—it was the unfolding capacity of the (open) organization to accomplish more than was ever hoped for initially. In other words, the campaign's potential was discovered rather than "designed."

The campaign was constantly shaped with the assistance of participants who were unpaid and geographically distant from the national headquarters and who were independent operators not accountable to the official campaign organization. Parallel structures and informal organizations blossomed. Such proliferation allowed competing visions and aspirations for the campaign to be entertained (also expressed in the overall goal of "Taking our country back"). Such open organizing thus escapes the trap of having to conform to one preconceived vision of the future—a state that Postrel (1998) has called the "enemy of the future" because it circumvents the processes of competition and experimentation in favor of preconceptions and prejudices. Let visions, not just strategies and organizational structures, also compete!

Open, participatory conceptions of organizing offer a way to escape the kind of dull-execution mentality that results from the top management team's setting the strategy while everyone else is called on simply to execute and meet the preset target goals (Bossidy, Charam, & Burck, 2002). Instead, through instances like the Dean campaign, organized activities become experimental playgrounds where the management task is creating the architectures of contribution so that the potential contributions of many participants are actualized and assembled into a joint effort rather than dissipated. Such an approach does not guarantee that the desired outcomes will be achieved (nor does any other kind of organizing by the way), but it invites more experimentation (and thus requisite variety) to find, when appropriate selection mechanisms are applied, the most promising avenues of action.

In conclusion, the cost of organizing is declining, and hence we can expect much more organizational action in the future. We are about to enter the age of open organizing and pervasive volunteer activity. Perhaps some of these virtual organizations will be short-lived and hence disposable; yet the underlying activity of committing to special-interest causes is likely to be highly resilient. For example, Sweden has recently seen the rise of the Pirate Party that opposes copyright restrictions on the Internet. Open organizing potentially combats this tendency for issue splintering. It is our hope that the global society does not fragment into groups of people with each group's being committed to a single cause and unable to converse with others. Resilience requires the accommodation of multiple viewpoints, even if some of us always would "want to have our company back."

POSTCARD NO. 3 FROM SAN JOSE, CALIFORNIA: TEMPERED RADICALISM AND MANAGEMENT PRACTICES THAT STICK

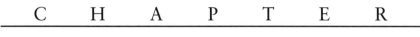

This next postcard, written with Robert Chapman Wood, talks about how to change large institutions (private companies and intergovernmental organizations such as the European Union) and what the effective strategies are for activists at any level of the organization.

ODD REVISITED

Ordinary professionals often don't know their own strength. A powerful yet little-studied way large organizations can innovate is for groups of activist managers and professionals to join together to change routines and alter taken-for-granted ways of thinking. The evidence suggests such activism can be far more powerful than most people—including activists themselves—realize. Such activism is gaining more attention (Meyerson, 2001). Kleiner (1996) wrote an early study. Rao (2009) recently published a book on market rebels. Activism is changing basic thought processes. It represents a new approach to enabling large, established firms to innovate [for example, Shell Oil (see Hamel, 1999)], quite distinct from strategic planning (Ansoff, 1988), reliance on "emergent strategy" (Mintzberg, 1990), or the deliberate chief executive decision making that journalists

This chapter is modified from an article by Robert Chapman Wood and Liisa Välikangas, "Managers Who Can Transform Institutions in Their Firms: Activism and the Practices That Stick," in *The SAGE Handbook of New and Emerging Approaches to Management and Organization*, edited by David Barry and Hans Hansen, SAGE Publications, Thousand Oaks, CA: 2008. Reprinted with permission from SAGE Publications Ltd.

often celebrate. Robert Wood of San Jose State University and I argue that activists who understand the political nature of institutional change can play key roles in enabling firms to meet environmental challenges. This will require, however, knowledge and skills that few activists have adequately demonstrated.

Activists need to draw on recent theory of institutions—the basic, taken-for-granted rules of the game in human systems. First, activists need to understand better the nature of institutions inside their organizations—that the institutions are automatically accepted as part of reality yet ultimately alterable and that they make it possible for activists to perform some vital tasks of renewal while making others enormously difficult. Second, activists need to understand the nature of institutional entrepreneurship. Institutional entrepreneurship theory shows how activists can carry out the difficult political tasks of bringing together constituents to support new ways of doing things and then getting people accustomed to ways just different enough to work.

AT&T's Opportunity Discovery Department (ODD) (the story that is told in full in Chapter 10) presents a good case in point. It became a hub for a sort of social movement (McAdam & Snow, 1997) in the organization aimed at rejuvenating it. Officially established to examine technology futures and develop tools for scientific strategy making, its people constantly promoted change they believed the firm needed to survive. They achieved remarkable, though partial, success. However, the firm's ultimate sale to SBC (which adopted the AT&T name) represented defeat of the venerable, pioneering company ODD sought to save.

Table 13.1 lists lessons from institutional theory and compares them to ODD's behavior and its results. We briefly consider the definitions of *institution* and their usefulness for practitioner challenges such as those faced by the ODDsters, suggesting an approach that we believe makes clear the institutional issues that activists confront. We then outline what institutional theory could have taught ODD and can teach activists elsewhere—practitioner-oriented understandings of institutions and deliberate institutional change. We compare what institutional theory teaches to ODD's behavior and draw new insights into institutions from ODD's experience.

Table 13.1 Key Lessons of Institutionalism for Activists

Topic	Literature	ODD Behavior	Results
Nature of institutions	Institutions are rules of the game (North, 1990) that are taken for granted (Berger & Luckmann, 1966) and that create a logic of appropriateness (March & Olsen, 1989).	ODD knew it was trying to change the rules, but it often took existing rules for granted in ways that hurt its overall project (for example, acting as an AT&T Labs–based support unit, it did not develop strategy for reaching top management).	ODD proved "right" in retrospect, but it did not ultimately succeed in transforming AT&T. Its work had significant impact on some parts, but it never built relationships with the managers most important to its success.
Nature of institutional entrepreneurship	Institutional entrepreneurship is highly political (DiMaggio, 1988).	ODD reveled in being different and using methods that were highly original (including unusual language). ODD was more like a rebellion seeking to awaken than a constitutional movement seeking political and institutional support.	While ODD survived as a movement for a surprisingly long time (perhaps due to its links to Bell Labs), it ultimately dissipated as its position became politically untenable and some of its leaders left.
Process of institutional change	Institutions are formed not so much by deliberate decision as by habitualization, objectification, and sedimentation (Berger & Luckmann, 1966).	ODD was successful in initiating some new management practices (such as scenario planning), but it failed to make these routine practice.	ODD never achieved substantial changes in strategy making at AT&T as a whole or got the core strategy-making efforts to take it, as an R&D unit, seriously as a contributor.
Institutional entrepreneurship skills	Supporters must form a "center" or "core" supporting new institutions through the skillful use of tactics such as agenda setting and "goallessness" (Fligstein, 1997).	Some ODD behavior was politically astute, but as it achieved successes, it did not develop a political strategy to build on the successes and its large grassroots network to consolidate its support.	Lack of a well-structured coalition and a senior executive's championing made it easy for enemies to kill ODD after its creator left the firm. ODD's revolutionary air may have also felt threatening to the AT&T "establishment" once ODD became seen as a potentially competent entity.

A SOCIAL MOVEMENT AS A RESPONSE TO AT&T'S PROBLEMS

AT&T was hobbled by institutionalized behavior that prevented it from changing and that the ODDsters represented a genuine social movement promoting transformation. To see a strategy as appropriate because it is the same as that of other firms in its industry is common in institutionalized organizational fields (Scott & Meyer, 1991), but it is inconsistent with success in competitive fields where many firms doing the same thing quickly turn a profitable product into a commodity (Porter, 1980). AT&T's planning resembled systems described in Grant (2003), who notes that they help firms adapt to turbulence but rarely support nonincremental innovation.

The response of Blonder, Muller, and their associates embodied each of the elements of McAdam and Snow's (1997) definition of a *social movement*: "(1) collective or joint action; (2) change-oriented goals; (3) some degree of organization; (4) some degree of temporal continuity; (5) some extra-institutional collective action." (We say the work represented extra-institutional action because it violated both official rules that defined ODD's tasks and informal understandings of what scientists and other low-level professionals did at AT&T.)

For survival, this movement required support inside AT&T's dominant coalition. Senior executives could have fired participants. However, there was good reason for many to support or tolerate the ODDsters' work. Though they had not created the means to address them, many senior executives did recognize that the company faced huge challenges. ODDsters, coming from Bell Labs, were given leeway to think about them.

ODD'S STRENGTHS AND WEAKNESSES

By 1997 ODD was making significant contributions. In May executives of AT&T's $26-billion-a-year consumer business asked ODD to help them develop a new strategy. The result called for migrating AT&T home users to AT&T Wireless as the sale of stand-alone long-distance became less viable. AT&T's chief executive, executive council, and board of directors all reacted favorably. Later the Business Network Services and wholesale business units also asked for ODD strategy help.

Thus the ODDsters had accomplished a great deal. They had brought focus to overwhelming problems. They were helping senior executives develop solutions.

However, ODD also had real weaknesses. What exactly was ODD trying to do? It was successfully calling attention to problems. However, if the goal was to encourage real business achievement, ODD did not seem to be addressing the whole of the challenge. ODD often seemed to take for granted much of the institutionalized system that marginalized researchers. When the ODDsters referred to a rising executive as an "empty suit" and sought to "infect" him, they were thinking like gadflies rather than players. A list of ODDsters' reflections on what they could have done differently (reprinted in Chapter 10) included "avoided an us-versus-them mentality that may have created some confrontation" and "turned down the ODDsters' slight intellectual snobbism" (Muller & Välikangas, 2003: 117).

ODDsters never developed a clear and coherent approach to top management or to the corporate strategy and planning department—although top management would inevitably have to lead the transformation they were seeking. (The reflections list also includes a statement that they should have "sought to address higher audiences in top management in a more systematic manner.") Moreover, ODDsters gave little thought to how to deal with challenges to their influence.

THE FALL OF ODD—AND AT&T

Building a movement around the knowledge of the dangers an organization faces is hazardous. People who understand your message may leave. During 1997, several key movement members left. As discussed in Chapter 10, the departures culminated in November when Greg Blonder left the firm soon after a journalist published his off-the-record thoughts about the future of network evolution. [He is now a prosperous venture capitalist (Blonder, 2005)].

The departures, especially Blonder's, put ODD in a vulnerable position just when it was achieving success that might have led to real power. Neither the head of the labs' research division nor the head of the corporate strategy and planning department supported ODD's work. The research division head who had approved the creation of ODD had left AT&T soon afterward. His replacement opposed general distribution of ODD analyses.

Competition destroyed long-distance telephone service as a business, and few other AT&T businesses succeeded. When SBC took over years later, the company operated under the AT&T name but with a completely different leadership from the firm where ODD had operated. The problems that ODD had recognized had destroyed AT&T as an independent corporation.

DISSIPATED POTENTIAL FOR REAL SUCCESS?

All the data suggest that ODD's campaign had potential for creating real ability to innovate. ODD moved strategic thinking in AT&T toward much better cognitive management. It involved the company's best experts in important strategic analysis and brought about careful examination of scenarios. It opened the organization to intelligent consideration of new ideas and the creation of credible new strategies for business units that had not had them. Within two years of its founding, it was surprising itself with its influence at the highest levels of the firm. Though opposition proved powerful, ODD clearly had potential to conceive strategic actions if not change them in ways that could have transformed its performance.

However, the case also shows the difficulties of achieving strategic transformation through a social movement. ODD spawned opposition not only from managers who had reason to fear loss of their power but from the new head of Bell Labs who took for granted the existing system. Equally important, the ODD movement suffered from difficulties likely to plague social movements of all kinds, including a lack of sophistication about political management. As mavericks, its members were inexperienced in or unwilling to deal with hierarchical power. They failed to plan for a workable coalition in the organization. While ODD's achievements were impressive, therefore, the unfulfilled potential of the movement was even greater.

ODD AS AN INSTITUTIONAL CHANGE EFFORT

ODD's story shows the urgent need for activist managers but also the profound difficulty of their task. Institutional theory can help address the challenges. To make it useful, this section discusses how to define *institution* for practitioners. We also use our definition to show why ODD should be understood as an institutional change effort. This allows the following section to show what the literature on institutions can teach practitioners and how ODD's experience can inform institutional theory.

Defining *Institution* So Theory Can Relate to Practice

The study of "institutions" is notorious for diversity of definitions, which hampers dialogue. Fortunately Scott (1994, 2001) has cogently argued that competing definitions point to more or less the same underlying phenomenon. He points to the fable of the blind men and the elephant—the man who feels the head defines the elephant as "like a pot," the man who feels the ear defines it as "like a winnowing basket." "Much of the disagreement among contemporary analysts," Scott says, "is because they are focusing on different aspects of this complex phenomenon" (1994: 56).

But Scott does not solve the definition problem for us because his definitions of *institution* are too complex to guide practitioners.[1] We need a simpler definition. If Scott is correct that the simpler definitions to a considerable extent merely capture different facets of what institutions are, to think clearly about institutional theory and practice, perhaps we can simply choose one of the standard simple definitions and treat others as providing additional information about the phenomenon.

Economics' standard definition is accepted by most institutional economists: "the underlying rules of the game" (North, 1990). Williamson (2000) shows it works at many levels of analysis. Moreover, to say that AT&T had difficulty because the "underlying rules of the game" failed to support strategic thinking and innovation effectively summarizes key aspects of why AT&T could not innovate. Other definitions could be used—for example, Oliver's (1997) definition: actions that "tend to be enduring, socially accepted, resistant to change, and not directly reliant on rewards or monitoring." However, while ODD *was* struggling with institutionalized activities as Oliver defines the term, to focus on the fact that strategy processes in AT&T were "enduring" and "socially accepted" seems to take us a step away from the issues important to practitioners.

Thus "the underlying rules of the game" is our definition of *institution*. But since differing definitions capture different aspects of the underlying reality, we will assume that the "underlying rules of the game" in human systems also normally tend to meet Oliver's definition. (They are "enduring, socially accepted, and resistant to change.") We also hypothesize that they fulfill Berger and Luckmann's (1966) definition ("reciprocal typification of habitualized actions by types of actors") and others.

Scott also makes another point central to drawing useful conclusions. He notes that institutions are the same phenomenon at many levels of society (2001: 55–60). Thus with appropriate caution we can use data and theory from different levels when examining any institutional phenomenon.

AT&T's Problems and ODD's Struggle for Institutional Change

The rules-of-the-game definition makes clear that ODD had to pursue institutional change. As discussed above, the prevalent rules of the game in AT&T blocked it from realizing the potential of its resources. Positioning its work as a crusade, ODD was inevitably pushing to change the institutions.

Despite a clear understanding of the basics of the problem, however, ODD lacked a comprehensive way to think about solving it. The members did not know how to think clearly about changing institutions. ODD was happy to be "odd"—to remain outside the power structures. To succeed in the activist's task, however, it needed more—the kind of social skill that brings new institutional forms into existence. Clear understanding of institutionalized rules and how they can be deliberately changed could have helped ODD and could help other practitioners as well.

INSTITUTIONAL KNOWLEDGE AND MANAGEMENT PRACTICE

This section outlines what practitioners need to know about institutions and deliberate institutional change (that is, changing the rules of the game). Strong evidence shows that better institutions can enormously improve social systems' performance (North, 1990; Oliver, 1997). But it has been challenging to identify how intentional behavior can improve institutions. Here is a summary of what recent studies show.

Sociologists and economists agree that institutions promoting less-than-optimal performance are common (see Part 2, "Step 1. Managing the Consequences of Past Performance"). Studies that shaped the "new institutionalism" in sociology and in economics had very different purposes, but they agreed on this (Meyer & Rowan, 1991; North & Weingast, 1989). North (1990) holds that most of today's emerging-market, underdeveloped countries are plagued by poor institutions. Thus, institutional issues as serious as AT&T's—with rules of the game that keep systems from improving—are common. But how can a concerned member or group—people with influence but not chief executive power—encourage positive evolution of institutions? There are good reasons to think recent studies can help activists answer this.

How Activist Managers Should Understand the Nature of Institutions

Changing institutions is difficult because of the very nature of institutions. A first step for managers who wish to learn from institutional theory is to understand that nature. Institutions are not just rules-of-the-game entities ["regulative structures" in Scott's (2001) terminology]. They are also taken-for-granted elements of people's thinking patterns (Berger & Luckmann, 1966). Moreover, they are "logics of appropriateness" (March & Olsen, 1989) that tell people what to do in certain kinds of situations. (Scott's terms for the Berger and Luckmann and March and Olsen types of understandings are "cognitive structures" and "normative structures," respectively.)

These faces of institutions are powerful sources of inertia that activists need to overcome. People with little or no obviously rational reason to oppose an institutional change (such as the AT&T Labs' leadership in 1997 and 1998) may create overwhelming obstacles just because they take existing ways for granted and deem them appropriate. Moreover, those who seek change can take existing institutions for granted as much as anyone else. The ODDsters' failure to develop politically necessary relationships with senior managers even when their successful annual planning document demonstrated the ODDsters' value, for example, may have derived in part from their tendency to take their institutionalized role as an AT&T Labs–based support group as given.

The Basic Processes of Institutional Transformation

Managers who understand the problem also need to understand the processes by which they can change institutions. A standard model describes a substantial part of this. New rules of a game become real through a process of first "habitualization," then "objectification," then "sedimentation" (Berger & Luckmann, 1966; see also Tolbert & Zucker, 1996). People start doing something a particular way, and that way seems to work. So they repeatedly do it that way (habitualization). When activities must be explained to others, particularly to people who join the system, they come to be seen as part of objective reality ("the way things are done around here"). That is objectification. Sedimentation is the completion of the process. The behavior becomes so taken for granted that it becomes a standard part of people's mental furniture.

For activists, however, the most difficult challenges occur before anything like habitualization can take place. How does a supporter of institutional change first get an organization to use new ways? DiMaggio (1988) describes the deliberate creation of institutional change as "institutional entrepreneurship" and each individual effort as an "institutionalization project." He argues that successful creation of new institutions "is a product of the political efforts of actors to accomplish their ends and that the success of an institutionalization project and the form that the resulting institution takes depend on the relative power of the actors who support, oppose, or otherwise strive to influence it."

To succeed, ODD had to carry out an institutionalization project itself or persuade others, higher in the organization, to do so. DiMaggio portrays the actors in such projects as having a relatively clear idea of changes they want to create, but this may not always be true. Some innovation-supporting institutions seem to emerge because someone improvises one big innovation, and then others try to learn from the process, generating a routine (Wood, Hatten, & Williamson, 2004). Whether new institutions are improvised or deliberately chosen, however, DiMaggio argues that goal-oriented struggles create them.

In these political efforts, innovation supporters have to develop a strong coalition for change. Some organized groups always have interest in maintaining institutions as they are. Innovators, moreover, have to overcome institutions' taken-for-granted nature. The ODDsters are examples of activists who probably did not pay enough attention to political processes. Their reflections on what they could have done differently (should have "sought to address higher audiences in top management in a more systematic manner") hint at weak political thinking. DiMaggio's argument suggests that (highly successful) activists are inevitably politicians.

Social Skills for Institutional Change

Fligstein (1997) expands on DiMaggio's model. He suggests that creating new institutions is a matter of having the right social skills—the "ability to motivate cooperation in other actors by providing those actors with common meanings and identities in which actions can be undertaken and justified." Fligstein focuses on an effort that built new international institutions. However, his analysis is equally relevant to activists in firms.

Fligstein discusses Jacques Delors, the former French finance minister who headed the European Union's governing body in the 1980s. Delors took the job when the European Union was in crisis. Its dissolution was being discussed. "Eurosclerosis" was considered a profound problem, and analysts doubted that European firms could compete with Japan and America. Delors and allies among EU officials sought a goal that had much in common with the goals of corporate activists: to open Europe to innovation through institutional and market reforms. Moreover, their means had direct parallels with those of the ODDsters. Delors and his associates worked to build what Fligstein and Mara-Drita (1996) call an "elite social movement"—a movement of officials, businesspeople, and others interested in overcoming Europe's problems. Indeed, when Delors joined the European Union, he joined a movement called the "Single Market Program" already launched in the EU bureaucracy by officials who, like the ODDsters, saw a need for change. It sought to radically reduce remaining European trade barriers. Delors's political skills invigorated the movement, and it succeeded. EU nations agreed to 264 directives in the name of the Single Market Program, eliminating taxes and barriers and harmonizing rules such as health and safety codes. The program went into effect in 1992, and Europeans became habitualized quickly. Moreover, innovation did increase and prosperity returned. The program's success allowed Delors to help create additional new institutions, including European monetary union.

Fligstein builds on this to present a new analysis of how politics can change institutions, which he calls "the political-cultural approach" (Fligstein, 2001). He describes processes and tactics that institutional entrepreneurs (Delors and the officials who worked with him) can use to remake institutions.

Traditional economics and much political science use rational-actor models of change. They see the emergence of new institutions as bargaining. Environmental change makes existing arrangements suboptimal, and actors, who have fixed preference functions, bargain to create new arrangements (Shepsle & Bonchek, 1997). These models are not useful to activists, who perceive problems that others do not yet see.

Fligstein, on the other hand, notes that often parties in a problematic situation do not understand each other's positions. Negotiations may be stymied because of their different perceptions. In this situation, institutional entrepreneurs may promote the emergence of a new "cultural frame" that will cause people's understandings and thus preferences to change. This is how institutional entrepreneurs bring about major change. Existing institutions and organizations "constrain and enable" actors, structuring what is possible. However, people's interests are not fixed. Institutional entrepreneurs give actors a new sense of their interests and thus support changes in the rules.

They can lead a redesign of areas that are unformed (new technical fields, for instance) or that are in crisis (like that experienced by Europe's markets in the 1980s). They succeed if they unite the right kind of core group to support something powerful and (to the entrepreneurs) worthwhile. "Strategic actors must find a way in which to bring together as many groups as possible to form a center or core," Fligstein (1997) says. By creating an appropriate "cultural frame," Delors and EU staff members made the Single Market Program appealing.

Fligstein notes that actors have to select from "a small number of tactics" to build a powerful core around an appropriate cultural frame. Among the tactics he discusses are these:

- *Agenda setting:* Getting people to agree on what will be talked about
- *Framing proposed actions:* Convincing people to think that what will happen is (a) in their interest or (b) natural, given values that they accept or should accept
- *Taking what the system gives:* Seizing unplanned opportunities, and seeing opportunities where others see only constraints
- *"Goallessness":* Appearing open to others' needs, free of values oriented to personal gain, not wedded to a course of action, and therefore an appropriate broker among others
- *Brokering:* Helping people with different attitudes to communicate and reach agreements[2]

Such tactics can bring together important people in the system to support a new way of thinking so that a new course of action can be adopted and institutionalized. Delors and his allies built a body politic in all Europe to support a reworking of Europe's market institutions using the tactics Fligstein discusses. He focused on agenda setting from the beginning, telling European leaders that he would take the presidency of the EU only if they committed to a big project and then quickly concluding after a tour of European capitals that the idea of "completing the single market" was the most popular alternative. Thereafter he had legitimacy to focus discussion on that. Delors and EU staff members framed the project as in the interest of all Europeans. Initially, there was essentially no definition of "completing the single market," but the idea of eliminating barriers and harmonizing regulations could be sold as a source of great efficiencies. Then shared belief in "completing the single market" could be used to persuade people to support changes they had previously opposed. Delors's relatively goalless attitude when he took the presidency gave him credibility. People believed he would have supported whatever big revitalizing project the leaders of the continent wanted. "Taking what the system gave," he allowed the existing European system and the movement that was emerging in support of change to set boundaries. Delors became a well-respected broker, finding aspects of market change that would appeal to each political group.

ODD also used tactics on Fligstein's list, and those tactics contributed to successes. Advocating scenario planning was a way for people with no formal authority to alter agendas. Scenario planning's standardized, non-partisan nature gave the scenario-planning experts an air of goallessness. ODD's willingness to take over activities such as the editing of newsletters was a tactic of "taking what the system gives."

However, ODD never used these techniques in a coherent approach to the political problem that DiMaggio and Fligstein have seen as central: creation of a core group powerful enough to truly change the rules. Fligstein never closely examined the EU officials whose role paralleled that of the ODDsters—the group that originally conceived the idea of a Single Market Program. But he has implied that they always recognized that their success would require finding major support at higher levels. If ODD had made slightly better use of Fligstein's tactics, it still might have failed. But there is every reason to believe there was also a possibility for great success.

ODD's Contribution to Institutional Knowledge

Although ODD did not achieve dramatic changes in the rules in AT&T, its partial successes strongly suggest that mechanisms of social movements can achieve great impact in organizations. ODD showed the power in a large organization of visions that start among less powerful people and then expand their reach outside hierarchical channels, of people making sacrifices for a cause, and of the use of catchy phrases and simple, some-times stylized facts to recruit new believers. In a world where many firms face rapid change that undermines traditional business models, social move-ments within organizations seem an effective way of using firms' accumu-lated knowledge to evolve in needed ways.

For this to happen, however, both activists and senior managers will have to learn from the experiences of ODD and other activist endeavors. ODD's experience shows that activists can easily learn to talk to and work with peers and with people just above them in the hierarchy. However, developing needed relations with senior managers may overwhelm them.

RESILIENT ACTIVISM

This analysis shows that there is reason to believe that activism and the social movements that activists build in organizations can contribute enormously to change in large firms. The movement that the Opportunity Discovery Department spawned made remarkable progress in encouraging evolution. It failed to achieve true transformation in part because activists simply did not understand or focus on processes of enrolling senior management in their vision. (Some blame is surely on senior management also in failing to develop the interest.)

Institutional theory provides credible guidance for activists on how to achieve the success that eluded the ODDsters. The challenge is fundamentally political: institutional entrepreneurship. Activists need to bring together strong groups of supporters including top-level executives.

Our knowledge of activism inside organizations remains rudimentary. We especially need case studies that are more theoretically informed than those published to date. Such research is needed because businesses need a better, more theoretically informed practice of activism today, when environmental changes clearly call for dramatic evolution. Business needs more theoretically informed practice on two levels. First is among activists themselves. They need to think through their political roles and tactics. The second, equally important, is among senior managers. If senior managers are to be in charge of the evolution of their firms, they need to look to activists to mobilize expertise, articulate possibilities, and play key roles in assembling coalitions. ODD was advocating and making progress toward creating genuinely different ways of thinking about the whole business. Theory provided no guidance to upper management in how to respond.

Activism has the potential to bring about desperately needed institutional changes in large established firms and to facilitate international collaboration. But much more work is needed by scholars, activists, and senior executives if the promise is to be realized.

POSTCARD NO. 4 FROM WOODSIDE, CALIFORNIA: THE CHALLENGE OF INVENTIVE EXPERIMENTATION TO MANAGEMENT RESEARCH—OR, WHO IS RESPONSIBLE FOR DEVELOPING NEW MANAGEMENT PRACTICE?

While the engineer who devises war instruments that may save his city is a worthy citizen, you would hardly permit him to marry your daughter.

—Plato, quoted in Gilfillan (1945: 72–73)

This postcard is a call for inventive experimentation by scholars and practitioners of management jointly. The development of management practice is too important to be abandoned by scholars. Such shared responsibility, I suggest, derives from three sources.

First, managers are often myopic (Levinthal & March, 1993). Not only do they (as people in general) learn vicariously, but they suffer from selection bias (Denrell, 2005): by focusing on winners alone, we may not realize that winners and losers may share the same characteristics (such as ambition), which then become hailed as "key success factors." It is also difficult as an insider to develop an unbiased view of the organizational environment in which one operates (Mezias & Starbuck, 2003).

Second, it does matter which management ideas get invented in the first place and eventually included in the repertoire of new and standard management practices. If a critical (life-saving) invention is not brought forward or is brought forward too late, consequences may be dire such as the disappearance of an entire civilization (Diamond, 2004). Or if the inquiry is done along lines that are blatantly wrong, the mistake may have lasting consequences as in the case of Soviet Union's falling behind in

This chapter is modified from a paper originally developed by Liisa Välikangas as a Woodside Institute Working Paper, Woodside, California, in 2006 and presented to the Organization Science Winter Conference in Steamboat Springs, Colorado, 2007 and to the Academy of Management, Anaheim, California, in 2008.

genetics due to the state dismissal of Darwinian theory of evolution (Futuyama, 2005: 537).

Finally, it appears ethically indefensible for those with (scholarly) knowledge to stay back and simply count the dead—that is, not intervene to develop the kind of management practices that would enhance the survival of companies, the productivity of employees, or otherwise benefit the economy. No matter what stellar research such a disinterested posture might produce, if it does not become translated into management practice, the knowledge remains academic.[1]

Of course, many scholars talk about the need to be "relevant." Some say research should be more immediately actionable (for example, Beer, 2001); others suggest scholars need to be more engaged with their subjects for mutual benefit (Van de Ven & Johnson, 2006). The impact on practice is not the sole criterion of excellence, of course, albeit management is presumably an applied art by nature (see, for example, Whittington, 2002). Many noninstrumental theories do help us understand the organizational reality in which we are situated and the institutional constraints that the very managerial actions in part contribute to creating. One should not be celebrated at the expense of the other, however. The two serve different functions: one the pursuit of knowledge and/or academic respectability, the other organizational goals and/or managerial legacy. But they, at a minimum, should act like agent provocateurs toward each other: incite rather than ignore or preach, catalyze (a priori) rather than describe and evaluate (a posteriori).[2] Regarding this need for interaction, a famous social scientist Kurt Lewin (1945: 132) wrote the following:

> The close tie between social research and social reality is one of the reasons why particular attention should be given to the practical prerequisites of field experiments and to the conditions under which social research leads to practical application. It seems to be difficult to "sell" even good social research to practitioners. As a rule, only if they themselves have been involved in the planning and execution of fact-finding, do the practitioners gain the insight and interest necessary for social action. The question how the expert can organize and assist lay-groups for fact-finding has, therefore, very great practical and theoretical importance.

Beyond any such assisted fact-finding or interchange (Warner, 1984), a higher standard still would be to charge management research with a mission to innovate, not merely document and analyze existing practice (cf. Mintzberg, 1979). An analogue from engineering sciences may be helpful here in describing the occasional invention stemming from long-term research efforts. According to an excerpt of transistor history:

> During one experiment [with germanium], [a Bell Lab scientist Walter] Brattain observed that a germanium crystal that was set in contact with two wires two-thousandths of an inch apart was amplifying. After exclaiming, "Eureka! This thing's got current gain!" he informed his colleagues that many years of research by many Bell Labs scientists finally paid off. They had invented the first semiconductor device that could do the work of a vacuum tube: the transistor. (www.lucent.com/minds/transistor/history.html)

Yet such a generative dance (Cook & Brown, 1999) between "years of research" and a novel tangible application has not become a welcome norm in management research (for example, Griffin & Kacmar, 1991), the way it has done so in engineering[3] where there are many labs for experimental research, and the students and faculty frequently cross academic boundaries to start companies and work in the industry. For example, at Dartmouth College, students regularly "build something," to prototype their idea or invention, as part of their class work.[4]

Similarly, tools, contexts, and activities or the very management processes and structures in which individual managers find themselves and their actions situated (see, for example, Oakes, Townley, & Cooper, 1998) can be innovated. Yet most potent implications may come when the management principles that govern organizations are themselves rethought. Barley and Kunda (2001) wonder about a postbureaucratic organization. The answer might call for management innovation—for example, experimentation around alternatives to an organizing principle like division of labor or a management principle such as hierarchical decision making.[5] There might be a need for inventing practices to embed "mindfulness" in an organization (Weick & Sutcliffe, 2001) or developing approaches to strategic planning that have a democratizing rather than stratifying impact

(Mintzberg, 1994; Hamel, 2002). Gary Hamel has recently called for management innovation to deliver "management moon shots"—that is, ambitious changes in management practice. Management innovation, while benefiting the work of a manager, can thus also contribute to determining which organizational characteristics are historical legacy and path-dependent happenstance and what are inescapable "laws" or first principles (Pfeffer & Fong, 2005).

That business schools lack management clinics is interesting. Much like medical schools have their clinical practices, perhaps business schools would also benefit from laboratories for studying and experimenting on management principles and practices systematically. Of course, many business professors do consult for companies much as medical doctors have private clinics, yet the business schools themselves are not vested in developing "new treatments" and clinical practices.

TOWARD INVENTIVELY EXPERIMENTAL SCHOLARSHIP

While invention and experimentation routinely take place in science laboratories, the norm in management scholarship has been away from such a pragmatist-inspired "productive inquiry" (Hickman, 1990) that would evoke an epistemology of practice—or knowing as action—rather than an epistemology of possession—knowledge as something possessed in the head (Cook & Brown, 1999). While the Cartesian in us may afford reasoning about the world, the Deweyan is poised to meddle with it, to try and change things (for example, Argyris & Schon, 1992; Lewin, 1945; Romme, 2003). Thus the inventive experimenter seeks not only to explain what has (already) happened (or tends to happen) but to open up the possibility for something *else* to happen. It is not being resourceful about the theoretical explanation to an existing, observed phenomenon (Dunbar & Starbuck, 2006). Rather, it is being inventive about the possibility of experiencing or creating different phenomena and sometimes variations of existing phenomena.

Perhaps experimental scholars could learn from venture capitalists. As one founder of a major Silicon Valley venture capital firm was admiringly described: "He is often wrong, but when he is right, he is really, *really* right." The role of an experimental scholar should be to entertain a portfolio of management innovations, much as does a venture capitalist, in full knowledge that many of these experimental innovations will soon fail but the portfolio as a whole will, with some luck, pay off. In science, such "portfolio building" is analogous to parallel experimentation (Chamberlin, 1890, 1897)—that is, the entertainment of multiple working hypotheses in an effort to increase the efficiency of experimentation and find unexpected or breakthrough results.

HACKING AT MANAGEMENT PROBLEMS

Many important management problems defy easy solutions. *Hacking*, a term currently associated with those occupying themselves with writing computer code, may be useful here as a metaphor for inventive experimentation.[6] Hacking may be particularly appropriate under circumstances in which the problem at hand, perhaps due to its rapid changing, is unsuited for a centralized, predetermined design (Postrel, 1998)[7] and/or in which the problem cannot—due to its internal complexity and conflict—be "solved" but only "worked at" (a distinction put forward by George Shultz in a conversation). Management innovation is such a problem.

Hacking represents the spirit of continuously and relentlessly chopping at a thorny yet meaningful or worthwhile problem, often through parallel and multiple efforts without the sense that such an effort one day will be finished. In other words, hacking is the antithesis of a typical preplanned "change management" program that begins ("unfreezes"), takes the predetermined actions, and enforces the new status quo ("refreezes"). Hacking also represents the spirit of "working at" management innovation—an effort likely to require tenacity and patience. Hacking brings the spirit of individual ownership of problems being worked at—hackers tend to address issues of meaning to themselves, typically to improve the features or efficiency of a software program that they consider important for their own use (Von Krogh, 2003).

PRACTICING INVENTIVE EXPERIMENTATION

Beyond *hacking* as a metaphor for the incremental, sustained approach of working at worthwhile problems, *inventive experimentation* is here defined as a commitment to the creation and prototyping of seemingly novel management actions, processes, and principles. Rather than a method, we might benefit from thinking of inventive experimentation as an *in vivo* laboratory, open to multiple methodological approaches. Much as chemists and biologists have their research laboratories and physicians practice medicine in their private practices, management scholars ought to engage in a diagnosis and treatment of management ills (see, for example, Howard, 1970) while allowing for the serendipitous discovery of new management ideas and principles in the process. Such a practice laboratory would consist of a cycle of invention and experimentation.

The antecedents for inventive experimentation can be found in action research (Clark, 1976, 1980) in that the work takes place in the crux between theory and practice. Here, however, the emphasis is less on participants' reflection on their experiences (Argyris & Schon, 1974) in a sense that the activity would seek to change or transform participant behavior through their learning or becoming competent in taking action and learning from it (Argyris & Schon, 1974: 4; Chriss, 1995). The emphasis I argue for is rather more on experimenting on practices that might work given the participant behavior as it is or that change the organizational context in such a way as to invite different responses. Hence it is the management context that is to be changed, not participant consciousness or competence. Another antecedent to inventive experimentation is clearly field experimentation; yet field experimentation is generally understood to perform a role of an assessor of the results of a particular program or activity (Weiss, 2000) rather than its inventor or shaper. It is thus a method for validation (rather than invention and exploratory experimentation).

INVENTION: EXPANDING POSSIBILITIES

The spirit of inventive activity, as mentioned before, is constitutive of new possibilities: to open up the opportunity for something new and potentially surprising to emerge (rather than seek theoretical explanations or causal linkages in something that has already happened). To the extent that this is approached consciously as an inventive rather than an imitative challenge, the act would require a search for original—perhaps on the fringe— approaches rather than copying what other companies may be doing (see

"Catalyzing Management Information," later in this chapter, for an example). Approaches for such invention vary immensely (from the storied "a thought in the shower" to more theory-driven, patentable inventions in engineering; for one account, see Wiener, 1993). Even though inventive methodologies lack scientific status, they should not be discounted as undesirable, making validation as a quest for knowledge more valuable or at least inherently more respectable than invention. Miner and Mezias (1996) argue that such "generative learning" that includes "an active, creative component" remains of crucial interest to "students of scientific invention, product development, and 'creative' organizations" while they acknowledge it represents formidable conceptual and modeling problems (p. 93).

What would support and catalyze inventive activities in management? A number of well-known concrete approaches are shortly recalled here in the pragmatic interest of inducing invention. First, approach the problem or issue through a different perspective or lens. This perspective can be a novel theory that might open up new ways of thinking about the issue. To the extent that the theory is predictive and operationable and thus formative of management behavior or structure, it could provide a useful tool for invention of an alternative management practice. What would this theory suggest is a good way to manage in a case appropriate to its predictions? Or we might test the limits of the theory. In what areas are its predictions brittle so that the experiments might be decisive in their impact? Or a shift in the point of view, such as customer's experience of purchasing and consuming the offering, might offer fresh ideas. For example, how might we facilitate the (lead) customer participating in the innovation process directly (von Hippel, 2005)?

Second, management inventors might study analogues. What can we learn from nontraditional organizations, perhaps outside the business world, in terms of the principles under which they operate? What can we learn from other institutions (for example, markets or cities) or biological processes (evolution of life forms) that could inspire us to think about how to manage differently, using an entirely different set of principles from what we have, presumably, inherited from the industrial age? For example, there is a line of research that suggests organizations—like living organisms—should manifest "requisite variety" (dating back to Ashby, 1956). Thus the challenge for scholar-inventors might be to invent management practices that would add variety to organizational life, perhaps by using some of the above analogues as sources of inspiration (see, for example, Jacobs, 1993).

In addition to expanding the imaginary space with different perspectives and analogues, management invention might benefit from a purposeful exposure of its underlying assumptions. What are the beliefs or norms that a particular management practice such as strategic planning builds on (see, for example, Mason, 1969)? Or the tendency of companies to reward people financially for innovation suggests that their belief, potentially misguided or detrimental in implementation, is that people innovate for pecuniary benefit. Identifying and setting aside, and thus neutralizing, some of these hidden, toxic, or orthodox assumptions is a first step toward an alternative conception of the issue at hand toward developing new management practice. According to Ghoshal and Moran's (1996) critique of the transaction cost theory, it offers a poor basis for management development as it builds on assumptions of human behavior not to be encouraged, despite or due to the fact that it appears, perhaps as a self-fulfilling prophecy, to explain organizational behavior to some extent (Frank, 1988; Bowie & Freeman, 1992). This raises an interesting question about the foundations of management development: whether the theories that best fit (current) reality are also the most desirable tools for developing new practice (or vice versa, see also McCloskey, 1988). Inventive experimentation might offer an avenue for building management practice on alternative, more preferable (Collins, 1997) theory grounds.

EXPERIMENTATION: LEARNING-BY-TRYING

Miner and Mezias (1996) in their review of organizational learning literature note that "surprisingly, there is almost no research explicitly addressing organizational experimentation in pursuit of inferential learning" (p. 93). They go on to note that while its importance has been noted by Argyris and Schon (1978), the conceptualization of such experimental learning and its distinct features are undefined. Dewey (1916), as quoted in Raelin (1997: 566), argued that "mere 'doing' or activity was not enough to produce learning; rather, doing should become a trying, an experiment with the world to find out what it is like." This is a radical departure from the notions of learning that seek to view learning as a game of stimulus response (see Weick, 1991, for a critique) where performance improves as behavioral routines befit consistency and reliability. In learning-by-doing, it is the accumulation of experience and the repetition of the activity that allows cost savings (for a critique, see Hall & Howell, 1985). Thomke (1998) has described experimentation in product development as an exploratory problem-solving methodology, used in the design and prototyping of new products.

As opposed to views on learning that are routine based, the concept of inventive experimentation proposed here is about reaching outside the established behavioral repertoire. Learning-by-trying is about doing something different—a variation indeed necessary even for learning-by-doing because, supposedly, the activities that can be improved upon must first be conceived or invented and trialed (Wood, Hatten, & Williamson, 2004). Yet there is little explanation as to where learning curves originate (Adler & Clark, 1991). Learning-by-trying thus may be a missing link in the literature of learning related to trial and error types of behavior (Miner & Mezias, 1996), pointing to the origins of novel, emergent routine behaviors.

Yet experimenting requires certain foolishness (March, 1978): the frequent failures to be expected should deter a reasonable person from learning-by-trying. Nevertheless, experimentation is often the only avenue for learning about something that is new and novel. First, experimentation allows the exploration of feasibility of the initial conception or invention. Building a prototype or running a pilot is a way to test the idea's practicality or its implementability. Second, experimentation invites the assessment and elaboration of the conception of the invention. Inventions often develop in a process of experimentation; they change and become reconceived, refined, or rejected. Third, experimentation is a way to learn about the management problem or issue at hand. Such direct experience with experimenting may help redefine the problem or issue by enhancing our understanding of its characteristics. Our exposure to and engagement with the experimentation may change "what now appears important" (March & Olsen, 1976: 80) to us, thus refining not only our conception or formulation of the problem but by impacting our preferences in seeking a redress. In a way, we are experimenting on ourselves, or at least our reactions to the emergent results of the experiment. Experimentation can of course take many different forms and designs (see "Catalyzing Management Innovation" at the end of this chapter for a variety of examples).

VALIDATION: ASSESSING THE KNOWLEDGE CLAIMS

Inventive experimentation is first and foremost proposed here as a way to simulate experience (March, Sproull, & Tamuz, 1991), not to validate causality. It is a tool for inviting serendipity by experiencing (more) possibilities and learning from them (by creating thick history)—thus making choices between experiences that have become "near histories." It is a tool for expanding the possibility frontier, thus making the experience endogenous. Experiences generated this way also help surface preferences, thus allowing the organization to learn about its own preferences and let them evolve in the process of experimentation.[8]

Inventive experimentation precedes validation as a knowledge quest. The purpose is to create interesting claims for scientific methodology to validate. Thus the purpose is not to assess the truth of any one knowledge claim; rather, this standard endeavor more suited for traditional research methodology in management sciences would naturally follow after inventive experimentation had run its course in the production of management innovation. *Then* it is the time to carefully formulate and test the emergent knowledge claims against hypothesized (and preferred) outcomes in a (controlled) management situation that may now be contextually better understood.

BENEFITS OF INVENTIVE EXPERIMENTATION

The nature of inventive knowledge claims is one of potential. Invention is imagining something else, or in Hanson's (1967) terms, we learn about the possibility of X (see Table 14.1). Such invention benefits from multiple (often idiosyncratic) methodologies and presents varied results. Nevertheless, this phase is crucial in expanding the population of possible hypotheses to be tested later in the knowledge creation process. Experimentation shapes inventions by considering their initial feasibility,

Table 14.1   Inventive Experimentation: The Nature of Knowledge Creation

Invention	Experimentation	Validation
Part of discovery: Learning about what is possible ("discover the possibility of *X*," Hanson, 1967)	Part of discovery: Learning about what is preferable ("discover whether *X*," Hanson, 1967)	Part of hypothesis testing: Learning about what is true (cause-effect) ("discover how to *X*" or "discover that *X*," Hanson, 1967)
Multiple methodologies; varied results	Often ignored as a phase in experimentation (March & Olsen, 1976); creative formulation and rough trial; possible recombination of multiple ideas	Established statistical methodologies; the focus of the scientific method
Searching for and/or inventing possible hypotheses to begin with	Considering "the reasons for suggesting [hypothesis] *H* in the first place" (Hanson, 1960)	Establishing "the reasons for accepting hypothesis *H*" (Hanson, 1960)
Example: A talent market inside a company	Example: A description of how such a talent market might work; followed by a rough test in practice that feeds the idea (hypothesis) elaboration	Example: More fully developed talent market hypotheses and trials

and in the process we learn about the nature of the problem we are tackling by reassessing its emergent characteristics and our preferences regarding the solution. Experimentation allows us to discover, again in Hanson's terms, "whether *X*": whether we have potentially a solution that is preferable to existing solutions. We may thus consider the reasons for suggesting a particular hypothesis, or an experiment, "in the first place." Validation is about accepting or rejecting a particular hypothesis using well-established scientific methodologies.

CONTRIBUTIONS TO MANAGEMENT PRACTICE

Inventive experimentation offers some benefits to management practice. Some of them, like the expansion of the set of managerial ideas or the inclusion of scholarly knowledge in the development of management practice, have already been referred to as motivations to inventive experimentation. Below I revisit the issue point by point:

1. *An agenda for management innovation.* What are the important management issues or problems to address today? Inventive experimentation would support the development of an agenda of management innovation, in collaboration with practitioners, in areas that scholars deem important to advance management practice on a sustained, nonaccidental basis (big, thorny management issues of timely importance such as the cost of strategic renewal or corporatewide innovation capability) and in areas that practitioners deem could make a difference to their capacity to manage. In addressing these important issues, inventive experimentation (to the extent it has institutional quality) would help make management innovation intentional and sustained, not merely serendipitous and occasional. An agenda, or a set of known "bugs," would support the persistent "hacking at" management problems by an open community of scholars and practitioners.

2. *Development of a portfolio of management innovations.* As it is unlikely that solutions to big management problems can be devised with one shot, inventive experimentation would help create a portfolio of ideas, experiments, and eventually emergent innovations that have desirable qualities. Such a portfolio would add variety to management practice, and to the extent radical ideas can be created and experimented on, it would contribute to the enlargement and substantial revision of the selection set of management practices. This would avoid myopia in management practice such that most practices are small variations of one theme, thus lacking real variety as a population of options.

3. *Creating a scholarly interest in management innovation.* Management innovations should not be the privilege of consultants or the lone responsibility of managers with an insider bias regarding the properties of their organizations. Such bias might be reduced should management innovation be open to the scholarly community, able to consider the circumstances from a comparative, and hence more objective, stance, and bring a wealth of knowledge to bear on the management problem. It is this mutual interaction and cross-influence—or harangue—that might supercharge management innovation and add to the quality of ideas being invented and experimented on.

4. *Accelerating the pace of management evolution.* Assuming that the set of management practices is an evolving one beyond current best practices (thus today is not "the end of history" in management, to abuse Fukuyama, 1992), inventive experimentation provides an avenue for potentially accelerating the pace at which management practices become invented, experimented on, rejected and/or reformulated, and finally selected for use by executives with an interest in improving their management effectiveness. By adding variety to the set of management practices to be experimented on and eventually selected from, inventive experimentation is also true to Donald Campbell's statement, "Science will develop most rapidly when the widest range of guesses is being tried." Such radical variety would presumably also eventually benefit management practice.

THE MERITS OF THE SCHOLARLY QUEST

Boland and Collopy (2004: 9) call for a shift in researcher attitude: "A design attitude views each project as an opportunity for invention that includes a questioning of basic assumptions and a resolve to leave the world a better place than we found it." Inventive experimentation shares this ambition, humble or not but at least caring, in seeking to make a difference. Here are some aspects that might merit the scholarly quest:

1. *Cultivating the gift of serendipity.* Beyond a problem-solving aspiration, there are some benefits to inventive experimentation that are desirable characteristics of knowledge production. The discovery of the new and perhaps unexpected is often serendipitous—without an intentional search for the particular happenstance but being alert and tuned in enough to take note. As earlier noted in this book, in the letter of January 28, 1754, to Horace Mann by Horace Walpole, the original serendipity storyteller (Merton & Barber, 2004), states that such "accidental sagacity" excludes any "discovery of a thing you are looking for." Yet as the story defines, such luck requires "sagacity" to see and interpret what one may have encountered.

Serendipity is a gift, but it requires conducive circumstances under which such discoveries may take place. Inventive experimentation develops a platform for such planning for the unexpected insight or discovery (potentially unrelated to the initial purpose of the experiment). It provides a playground or a setting for observation, and therefore it is well placed to receive the gift that serendipity has to offer. Should there be multiple experiments in parallel, serendipity has a larger arena in which to make an appearance under the focused attention of the experimenter.[9] Inventive experimentation is a quest, and there is an implication that serendipity is the natural companion for quests of various kinds and requires alertness and good judgment. The Princes of Serendip were poised for discovery, accidental and otherwise.

2. *Beyond the retrofitting of theories—testing the limits to our knowledge.* Management research has been criticized for its backward-looking posture:

> One problematic consequence of researchers being able to choose what they study has been a focus on the past (Starbuck, 2006). Data are always retrospective, and theories consistent with retrospective data may not describe the future or even the present. In a challenge to the usefulness of such research, Platt (1964) argued that theoretical progress depends on confronting theories with crucial experiments that rule out unproductive lines of thought. Because researchers can craft retrospective theories to make them consistent with prominent stylized facts, these theories never appear utterly inadequate, and so testing them never rules out unproductive lines of thought. To expose the limitations of theories, organization researchers and designers alike have to use theories to predict and then they have to verify whether what happens corresponds to what they predicted. Organization design is an important and interesting area because it requires designers to make predictions, and it then generates evidence about the extent that predictions prove out in practice. (Dunbar & Starbuck, 2006)

McKelvey (1997) suggests paradigm proliferation in organization science is due to the difficulty of refuting competing claims across paradigms as they are not testable. While the purpose of inventive experimentation is not focused on testing predictions of existing theories in practice, it does offer an avenue for playing out the implications of current management theory in specific experiments.

However, to create such experiments in the first place often requires an experimental and inventive attitude (as in organizational design). Being forthcoming with the testable implications invites scholars to hack at the limits of their knowledge. The motto "If you think you understand something, try and change it" (in the spirit of Kurt Lewin and Bill Starbuck) illustrates the difference between personal engagement (Van de Ven & Johnson, 2006; Hanson, 1972) and detached ex-post analysis. Experimentation (or changing what we think we understand) can thus be an avenue to discovering the limits to our knowledge. (For example, in the famous Hawthorne experiment, the puzzle about productivity increases exposed misconceptions of worker motivation.) But it can also be a tool for eventually expanding that understanding (by experimenting on what we do not yet understand).[10] Thus experimentation allows us to expose the limits of our knowledge; it is also a methodology for exploration and the learning of new things. (Children, for example, experiment constantly.) Or in Weick's (1989) terms, experimentation helps us both create (a need for) theory as well as (in)validate it (or its laden hypotheses).

3. *Evolving judgment criteria (or, the endogeneity of the desirable).* Inventive experimentation will also help redefine the problem at hand. In contrast to Donald Campbell's view on experimentation as a methodology for validation (see Weiss, 2000), James G. March has emphasized the unexpected discovery of new goals and preferences as a consequence of social experimentation: the problem definition may change. As March and Olsen (1976) wrote in a paragraph that makes the experimenter an engaged participant:

> In particular, the evaluation of social experiments need not be in terms of the degree to which they have fulfilled our a priori expectations. Rather we can examine what they did in terms of what we now believe to be important. The prior specification of criteria and the prior specification of evaluational procedures that depend on such criteria are common presumptions in contemporary social policy making. They are presumptions that inhibit the serendipitous discovery of new criteria. (p. 80)

Experimentation thus engages, and even occasionally challenges, the normative beliefs of the experimenter as to what should be experimented on in the first place! Such experimentation will thus help redefine the issue at hand and its major or important characteristics. Should we accept not only the challenge of serendipitous discovery but also its potential impact on our scholarly beliefs, we have created, arguably, the ultimate conditions for involved scholarship. Indeed, we as scholars, apply ourselves in the experiment.

Such evolving judgment criteria may also help uncover and escape theoretical orthodoxy, including the choice of applying a particular theoretical framework to a research situation in the first place (when another framework could potentially yield much more inventive results). While the framework or theory may appear endogenously desirable—the scholar has a tradition of research in this area or the journals tend to look upon publications within this framework favorably—the very framework may be the barrier against alternative hypotheses. Furthermore, as certain research traditions become established, they become desirable as entry points for young scholars looking to build their scholarly reputations. This desirability may be entirely endogenous (that is, grown within) to the scholarly community, however, who through a peer-review process assess the validity of a research paper (leaving managers, journalists, and other societal stakeholders out of the evaluation). This is not to say that the academic community is not the right audience to assess a scholarly contribution; it is, however, to acknowledge that this assessment is exclusive[11] and is not subject to the test of other, exogenous, criteria (like practitioners' views).

RESILIENCE AS INVENTIVE EXPERIMENTATION

What inventive experimentation is not, is starting another consulting organization but rather creating a *laboratory* for management innovation. Inventively experimental scholarship is proposed as a sincere, altruistic pursuit of knowledge that aspires to contribute to, and potentially accelerate, the evolution of management practice by developing and trialing promising management concepts and/or inventions.

In Table 14.2, there is a summary of the assumptions behind inventive experimentation as a knowledge creation approach. As a strategy, such inventive experimentation would likely serve management research by supporting ambitious or interesting idea creation and theory construction. Circumventing the steps involved in invention and experimentation, it is proposed here, has been costly to management research, making the work

Table 14.2 The Assumptions behind Inventive Experimentation

Assumptions	Invention	Experimentation	Validation
There are scholars who can be inventive enough to create new management ideas and applications.	Variety in management practices is beneficial.	There is value to a portfolio of management innovations being experimented on.	Inventive experimentation helps assess the predictive claims of existing theories and contributes to the creation of new theories.
Management innovation benefits from a hackinglike attitude: a sustained effort to tackle important, difficult problems.	Invention, rather than imitation, is key to accelerating management evolution.	Problems become defined and redefined in the process of experimentation, providing learning.	Inventive experimentation helps create interesting hypotheses for validation.
Collaboration between academics and practitioners is beneficial to management innovation.		Experimentation allows the serendipitous discovery of the unexpected.	
Executives will see a benefit in inventive experimentation.		Experimentation allows us to learn about our assumptions and preferences. In vivo experimentation yields different kinds of insights than does in vitro experimentation.	

less innovative than it could have been. In Donald Campbell's terms, we have become mere assessors of the effectiveness of certain practices or programs. However, managers do not (often) intentionally set out to invent new management practice either. Rather, such activity appears to be serendipitous, not planned (see Birkinshaw, Hamel, & Mol, 2005).

Partly to blame, perhaps, is a methodological mindset. By rushing into the comfort of validation as the acceptable tool (Lindblom, 1987; Weick, 1996), a researcher is confined to refining the existing knowledge claims, shortcutting his or her capacity to be imaginative in creating interesting ideas to begin with (Weick, 1989; Hanson, 1960). Should the objection be that such inventive experimentation is the job of (open-minded) managers or the work of (occasionally mad) inventors and (frequently failing) entrepreneurs, not scholars, I would conjecture that it is not good enough for scholars to sit back and wait and see what works. Scholars need to get in the act of innovation and experimentation. Among managers, it is the instinctive mode, despite the evidence that local knowledge is sticky (Szulanski, 2003), to study best practices: What do other (well-performing) companies do about this? How do they manage the issue? Through inventive experimentation, inventor-experimenters, scholars, and managers alike can enrich or add to the quality and potential of management experience we can learn from.

An increasing interest in outlier performance (Lewin, 1989) suggests a frustration with studying the best practice (or the average and the aggregate) and may help drive inventive experimentation. Yet ultimately, inventive experimentation is motivated by the inventor-experimenters' desire, indeed compulsion, to invent and tinker with management practices. Let us hope there are more than a few inventor-experimenters among us, because—to paraphrase Karl Popper—if we do not experiment, we become the experiment.[12]

CATALYZING MANAGEMENT INNOVATION: AN EXAMPLE

To illustrate, I will relate an exercise that was specifically aimed at catalyzing management innovations at a U.S. retailer (see the full case study in Chapter 9, "Resilience in Action—Building Reservoirs for Change"). In one instance, the company engaged a group of people in an effort to invent management practices that would reduce the perceived role of "bureaucracy" as an impediment to its capacity to change. During the "Management Innovation Jam," as the workshop was called, the participants were first introduced to the challenge of smooth renewal (or strategic resilience). Inspiration was drawn from analogues: what may we learn from the principles of resilience in analogues such as life (evolution), cities, markets, or democracy that gives these systems a capacity to change?

Bureaucracy, or compliance mentality run amok and the yielding of individual responsibility and initiative to overly specified management process or organizational systems, had previously been identified as an impediment to change in the company. The participants then considered, in some detail, how bureaucracy in their experience had impeded them from taking necessary or desirable action (and how they themselves, inadvertently, may have contributed by their own behavior to the bureaucracy in some instances). Each told a story about his or her personal experience. They then moved, in small groups, to tackle one example that felt most compelling and explored the specific instance regarding its bureaucracy-related impediments. They discussed how the impediments may have been embedded in the company's beliefs and values, existing management processes and systems, and individual actions and behaviors, for example.

After these considerations, the small groups were "prescribed" a principle of resilience (for example, individual autonomy or resource flexibility) that they should "apply" to try to innovate around one of the impediments they had identified (see "The Management Innovation Exercise" sidebar). Their task was to come up with as many innovation ideas as possible. (The participants were also given stepwise guides to work through these questions.) The suggested ideas ranged from systemic notions such as the degree of implied (lack of) trust in management processes to more experimentable concepts of alternative resource allocation methods.

THE MANAGEMENT INNOVATION EXERCISE

Task 1: Pick one impediment. Based on the prior discussion, choose the bureaucracy-related impediment that your team considers most damaging to the company's resilience.

(continued)

Task 2: Consider the resilience principle you have been prescribed, and describe what happens when you apply the principle to the company's (a) beliefs and values, (b) existing management systems and processes, and/or (c) day-to-day actions and behaviors as you have just diagnosed them (or ask for another prescription if entirely inapplicable).

Task 3: Ideate. How might you change the company's management practice and/or work environment so that the resilience principle would contribute to the company's capacity to change without crisis?

This exercise may be classified as consulting to the extent that there were outsiders involved as initiators or facilitators. (However, the company in question had also engaged in this exercise without outsiders.) Scholars may critique on and ponder the premises of the work or study the outcomes. But inventively experimental scholars ought to participate in the context in which this type of management innovation takes place and share the responsibility in the quest. How should a company go about innovating its management practices (to support resilience or any other goal) assuming competitor imitation or serendipitous change (March, 1981) is not sufficient? The question relevant to scholar-inventors is, how to create and contribute to an appropriate, fruitful context for the invention and experimentation.

TYPES OF EXPERIMENTS

1. *Lead-user experiment:* Running an experiment with a small number of lead users

   Example: "eBay for HR," an in-company experiment to invite the most passionate employees to donate some of their time to causes they found worthwhile and work on the projects of their choice voluntarily

2. *Expert contest:* Inviting teams of experts to compete on a task
   Example: Forming multiple R&D teams to create a healthy cookie (See The Bake-Off by Malcolm Gladwell, www.gladwell.com/2005/2005_09_05_a_bakeoff.html.)
3. *Web-based open participation:* Harnessing contributions from a large number of people through a Web application
   Example: Predicting the sales of gift cards for the holiday season (See Hamel & Breen, 2007.)
4. *A physical prototype:* Creating a physical representation of the experiment (such as a prototype or a showcase)
   Example: Setting a desk in the cafeteria and inviting people to come and submit ideas as their "personal idea banker" (See Chapter 9, "Resilience in Action—Building Reservoirs for Change.")
5. *Time-compressed activity with a mission:* Dedicating a specific time window (such as one day) to accomplishing a particular goal
   Example: The FedEx Day (See the Atlassian, http://blogs.atlassian.com/rebelutionary/archives/000495.html.)
6. *Skunkworks:* Running a longer-lasting, small-scale activity on the fringe and/or under the radar
   Example: SunRay at Sun Microsystems (See Chapter 5 for a case study.)

BRIDGING THE RESILIENCE GAP

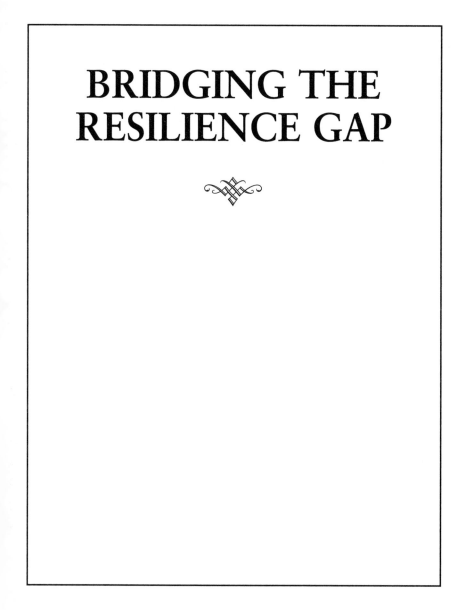

Can resilience be built from such engagement strategies as described in the four "resilience postcards" in the preceding chapters? It is my hope that such strategies will play an important part in closing the resilience gap—today's organizational capabilities and tomorrow's need for resilience—and will sustain the rise of the resilient organization.

Amateurs have throughout history been making significant contributions to technological and societal progress as the first postcard puts forward. Organizations open to contribution (as described in the second postcard) to anyone anywhere are likely, to the extent the effort can be effectively (self)coordinated, outcompete any closed system if they can, like the Dean for America (and later the Barack Obama) campaign, motivate a social movement type of enthusiasm behind their cause. (The Dean campaign did not fail because of its openness—even in the last stretch the informal organization fought hard for recovery.) Our institutions in Europe and the United States (as well as elsewhere in the world, like China) will need to adjust to future challenges, and for this purpose, tempered, institutionally savvy activism is critical as prescribed in the third postcard. Finally, in the fourth postcard I argue that management principles and practices are in dire need of inventive experimentation to rise to meet the global challenges that will require supreme organizational resilience. Inventive experimentation would help corporations and public institutions develop the advance change capability that is likely needed for the next 10 to 20 years.

Table C.1 suggests some of the impending challenges we need to face, together with my hope for emergent resilient responses. I suggest we start giving these issues serious thought. Because the encounters they produce are likely to require more than on-the-spot handling, they require the development and practice of resilience *now*. For instance, how will the increasing numbers of young, unemployed (and often unmarried) men find constructive purpose in life? In the Middle East, the youth unemployment rate (for

Table C.1   Resilient Responses to the Challenges Ahead

Big Challenges Ahead	Resilient Responses
Extreme religious-political movements	Tempered by international collaboration and culture of moderation?
Lots of unemployed young men	Surge of entrepreneurship and business venturing?
Radical changes in Earth's climate	Technological tidal wave?
Undepressable desire to grow rich in China	New global and social responsibility?
Global pandemics in disease, finance, fashion	Global institutional governance?
Growing urbanization	The fast spread of innovation in cities?
Aging of population in developed countries	A voice of tolerance and mature wisdom?
Virtualization of work (and some kinds of fun)	Increased reach and productivity?
Accentuated economic cycles	Instant morphing (mirroring of change)?
The increasing isolation of the superrich	Rise of the middle class in emerging countries?
Social media domination in (credible) communication	Reformation (and reinstitution) of authority?
Guerrilla warfare and issue-fighting tactics	Multiplication of decentralized, open organizations?
Global fragmentation of political power	Newly found consciousness and activity for sustainability?

those between the ages of 15 and 24) averages between 20 and 25 percent (Dhillon & Yousef, 2009). In China, there are some 120 men to every 100 women. At the minimum, women will need to highly resilient! And global pandemics—viral as well as financial—will tax every resource we have.

Throughout this book, I have called this proactive, forward-looking style *strategic resilience*. While resilience is a matter of management, it always includes some luck too. The rise in resilience as a management strategy is the topic of this book.

My central thesis is that resilience is something that needs to be rehearsed, not just planned for. Resilience is similar to being in shape. With senses alert, strong powers of observation, poised composure, and lots of life energy: that defines organizational vitality too.

Said a manager in a leading U.S. corporation in a quest for resilience:

> Resilience is like a muscle—we will need to build it so that we have it when the tiger is on our tail.

Therefore, it is necessary now to stop reading about resilience and start rehearsing it. I propose the next step in our resilience journey is to observe and record instances of resilience that are already, most likely, taking place in your organization. Capture these instances and write them on a postcard. Share this postcard with your colleagues. Send it to them and talk about why the particular instance in organizational life shows resilience (or lack of it).

FROM READING RESILIENCE POSTCARDS TO SENDING SOME

Write your own resilience postcards. Remember, resilience is not a strategy; it is a rehearsal. In fact, it is constant practice. I propose that you, together with your colleagues, start sending resilience postcards to each other. They can simply reply to these questions:

1. Tell us about an instance where you believe someone in your organization, or your organization all together, has shown resilience.
2. Why do you think so? What struck you as particularly resilient in that situation?
3. How can such resilience be rehearsed more widely in your organization?

You may wish to ponder also the following three questions, perhaps on your own and with your team:

1. How resilient do you believe your organization to be more generally, beyond this particular instance?

2. How would you like to show personal resilience?

3. Where have you observed or read about the most admirable resilience you'd like your organization to manifest?

In assessing the resilience of your organization, you may wish to consider the instances of resilience your organization has shown: How many opportunities are being pursued that have stemmed from an unanticipated market change? How strategic is the pursuit—that is, to what extent do these instances have the capability to renew and refresh corporate mission and strategy? Do they build reservoirs for change for the future? How many market changes have been missed that now pose a potential competitive threat in the past three to five years?

RESILIENCE ASSESSMENT

1. How many market changes have been identified and pursued during your tenure in the company?

2. What is the capacity of these pursuits to refresh corporate strategy and mission?

3. What kinds of reservoirs for change does the organization have for the future?

A CULTURE OF RESILIENCE

When you run to catch a cab, your heart rate accelerates—*automatically*. When you stand up in front of an audience to speak, your adrenal glands start pumping—*spontaneously*. When you catch sight of someone alluring, your pupils dilate—*reflexively*. *Automatic, spontaneous, reflexive*. These words describe the way your body's autonomic systems respond to changes in your circumstances. They do not describe the way large organizations respond to changes in their circumstances. Resilience will become something like an autonomic process only when companies dedicate as much energy to laying the groundwork for perpetual renewal as they have to building the foundations for operational efficiency.

—Gary Hamel and Liisa Välikangas (2003)

Resilience needs to become second nature. Part of this automatic, spontaneous, reflexive act requires managing the consequences of past performance so that the organization does not remain a captive to its past (see Part Two). Resilience requires building an organization that is receptive to its foundational ingredients: requisite (imaginative) thinking, resource scarce innovation, robust design, adaptive fitness, and *sisu* as discussed in Part Three. It is not a one-time effort. Rather, resilience requires constant rehearsal and management practice, as suggested in the final section of this book. Only then will resilience become the most sustaining of all, a part of the culture.

Resilience, like life, comes in different colors and shapes. There is the *tiger-on-your-tail* kind of need for resilience. The life-threatening situation in which you have to run as fast as you can. There is also the kind of resilience that sustains the company in between strategy shifts. Is your company in the process of implementing a new strategy? Trying to accomplish transformation? Most companies are, most of the time. So the second need for resilience is the *capacity to sustain strategy change*. The third kind of resilience is perhaps the most advanced—it is *the opportune*: turning threats into opportunities *prior to* their becoming either. Being serendipitously sagacious.

GOT RESILIENCE?

1. Can you outrun the tiger (that is, escape from or recover from a crisis)?
2. Can your organization thrive in between strategies?
3. Can you turn potential threats into opportunities prior to a specific threat materializing or the opportunity becoming heavily competed?

Endnotes

PART ONE

1. See Sevón and Välikangas, "Of Managers, Ideas, and Jesters" (2009). It appears to us that ideas are often much more powerful than people who tend to succumb to their persuasion and act out or perform these ideas. People often act in the name of some idea. Ideas also tend to live longer than people do (think of such persisting ideas as freedom or communism or fast food). You may wish to ask: Which ideas command you? What ideas are you performing? Which ideas have become you or your organization?

CHAPTER 2

1. Profits of the Fortune 500 companies were down 84.7 percent in 2008 compared to 2007 (*Fortune*, May 4, 2009: 137).

CHAPTER 3

1. The converse is often true too: an executive who has been badly burned, almost losing his position, as a result of investing in a particular country will never again entertain the idea of investment in that country. This is a sort of overlearning, or a Vietnam syndrome: never again, another Vietnam War.

CHAPTER 5

1. Oracle Corporation acquired Sun Microsystems in 2009 in competition with IBM.
2. Liisa Välikangas, Martin Hoegl, and Michael Gibbert, "Why Learning from Failure Isn't Easy (And What to Do About It): Innovation Trauma at Sun Microsystems," *European Management Journal*, 2008. Reprinted with permission.
3. Data were stored at a server where they were centrally managed, which rendered the computer box in the office just a dummy terminal.
4. "Sun Ray is one of the coolest—but most poorly marketed—products I've seen in 20 years. The idea that anyone can insert his employee badge into any computer in the world and watch his own desktop appear on the screen instantly is astounding. Show the world what you [Scott McNealy] showed me in your office in December, and Sun will rise again."
5. The success of a particular innovation such as Sun Ray is subject not only to competence and hard work but to luck, timing, and serendipity. An innovation that fails may eventually succeed as conditions outside the innovator's control change (such as the emergence of complementary technologies or the maturing of user attitudes).

CHAPTER 6

1. I thank Professor Yves Doz for feedback on this piece. I am grateful for many conversations around the notion of creeping commitment. All shortcomings are of course mine.
2. Ashby's law of requisite variety: The larger the variety of actions available to a control system, the larger the variety of perturbations it is able to compensate. Or, only variety can destroy variety.
3. I am grateful to Matti Copeland of Helsinki for suggesting this method as a way of making "intelligent decisions."

CHAPTER 7

1. A South African story told to me by Michael Gibbert.
2. This is an excerpt from an online blog published by the *MIT Sloan Management Review* in 2009 by Michael Gibbert, Liisa Välikangas, and Martin Hoegl.
3. Sometimes robust organizations are equated with high-performance organizations, but this raises the questions of over how long a period and across what kind of environmental change.

CHAPTER 8

1. This is a well-known Finnish word that denotes determination, perseverance, and ability to continue in the face of adversity.
2. See Gibbert, Hoegl, and Välikangas (2007). See also Välikangas and Gibbert (2008).
3. With warm thanks to Arne Carlsen for many great conversations and references to M. M. Bakhtin.
4. See also Koestler (1967).
5. See Sevón and Välikangas (2009).
6. Also *harlequin, jongleur, fou, narr, stultor, scurra,* . . . and more.
7. http://idler.co.uk/features/you-have-to-be-mad-to-work-here/.

CHAPTER 9

1. Not all ideas progressed to the experimental stage, of course. There were some ideas that did not prove worthwhile after reflection, and a handful of teams gave up the effort due to a lack of time (or possibly interest). Teams varied in terms of heterogeneity but generally had members from two to six different functional departments.

CHAPTER 10

1. Amy Muller and Liisa Välikangas, "An 'ODD' Reaction to Strategy Failure in America's (Once) Largest Telco." Reprinted from the *European Management Journal*, vol. 21, no. 1, 2003, with permission from Elsevier. We thank Paul Merlyn for contributing to this article.

2. Following the 1996 trivestiture of AT&T, the AT&T Bell Labs research staff was divided among the residual AT&T and the newly divested Lucent Technologies. Lucent's (now Alcatel-Lucent) research group retained the name Bell Labs. However, the company later announced it was withdrawing from basic science. AT&T's research group adopted the name AT&T Labs.

3. AT&T's corporate strategy and planning (CSP) department was not unlike the strategy organizations of many large traditional companies. The group was headed by an executive vice president who reported to the CEO, and his staff managed the extensive "process" of strategy making: largely guiding and collecting input and projections from the various business units as compiled by the group's strategy staff. A "consolidated" view of the strategy would emerge each spring and was discussed and reviewed by the executive team.

4. And this was before Skype!

CHAPTER 11

1. Liisa Välikangas and Quintus Jett, "The Golden Spur: Innovation Independence." Reprinted from *Strategy & Leadership*, vol. 34, no. 5, 2006: 41–45, with permission.

CHAPTER 12

1. Currently at Rutgers University.

CHAPTER 13

1. Scott's (2001) definition is: "Institutions consist of cognitive, normative, and regulative structures and activities that provide stability and
   meaning to social behavior."
2. The other tactics on Fligstein's list are direct authority (use of existing hierarchical power), wheeling and dealing (shaking up a situation
   to see where it ends up), asking for more than you think you can get,
   maintaining ambiguity, "trying five things to get one," aggregating
   interests, convincing people you hold more cards than you do, making others think they are in control, and framing actions in terms of
   the dominant groups to gain benefits from the system without disturbing those who are dominant.

CHAPTER 14

1. Presumably, the writings of management scholars have some impact
   on what managers do or how they think, at least to the extent they
   become known to managers (for example, Michael Porter's "five
   forces"—for a critique, see Knights, 1992). Therefore, by default,
   management scholars cannot remain as entirely detached parties, but
   they at least need to recognize this potential influence. Accepting
   responsibility would lead to a questioning of the nature of this influence: Does management research, for example, catalyze or suppress
   management innovation? Does it accelerate the pace at which management innovation happens over time?
2. Not only should management research have catalyzing consequences
   for management practice, but also management practitioners should
   be informed enough of scholarly work that an educated discourse
   between the two becomes possible. It is not in the scope of this chapter to suggest ways in which managers can become better informed
   of management research but instead to focus on the challenge to the
   management researchers.
      Suffice it to say that apparently widespread MBA education, the
   global industry of executive education, and *Harvard Business Review*

do not seem to be able to bridge the perceived divide (see Anderson, Herriott, & Hodgkinson, 2001; Rynes, Bartunek, & Daft, 2001). Many academic authors lament the lack of interest in management theory on the part of the practitioners. Few academic journals are read by managers.

3. Here is how Stanford School of Engineering seeks to attract students: "A compelling aspect of engineering is the joy of making things work: remote medical imaging that saves lives; or nanoscale structures that create remarkable new materials. Stanford offers space to investigate, design, and create in an unsurpassed arena of labs, research centers, and affiliate programs" (http://soe.stanford.edu/prospective_students).

4. According to a conversation with Professor Quintus Jett, Dartmouth College.

5. An alternative, experimental principle here could be self-coordination through transparency of action.

6. It should be noted that *hacking* is a significantly different metaphor or description of innovation than a traditional two-stage model of initiation and implementation (for a review, see Glynn, 1996: 1095), perhaps more in line with Amabile's (1988) point that no such smooth or linear steps exist.

7. "[U]nplanned, open-ended trial and error—not conformity to one central vision—is the key to human betterment. Thus, the true enemies of humanity's future are those who insist on prescribing outcomes in advance, circumventing the process of competition and experiment in favor of their own preconceptions and prejudices" (www.dynamist.com/tfaie/).

8. Experimentation can then be a tool for understanding the consequences of our (potential) choices better (as our preferences may change as a result of such experimentation). For example, an experiment entertaining a fully participatory organization could find out whether people actually like being totally "empowered" after having experienced it rather than merely envisioning it, and what (some of) the potential consequences of such empowering might be. The second experiment, a more elaborate one, can then benefit from the experience of the first, inventive, one. Finally, the third phase of

experimentation can seek to validate the fundamental proposition or the hypothesis, now more fully discovered, that forms the purpose of the experimentation.

9. It is important to make the distinction that inventive experimentation is about the discovery (or invention) of the new or heretofore unknown rather than validation of any particular existing knowledge claim. Hence serendipity can be properly and effectively harnessed to inventive experimentation whereas it is reasonably seen as the enemy of experimentation that is in search of validation. Control groups in the latter pursuit are particularly designed to exclude effects that are serendipitous.

10. Hanson (1967) describes these opportunities for discovery thus: (1) *Trip-over discovery:* The experimenter has no theoretical expectation for the discovery (accidental or serendipitous). (2) *Back-into discovery:* The experimenter has a theoretical expectation against the discovery (anomaly: Kuhnian paradigm shift). (3) *Puzzle-over discovery:* The experimenter has the full theoretical expectation for the discovery (a Eureka! moment).

11. It should be emphasized that such a statement is not an invitation to "bad science" but rather an opening for inventive experimentation that does not aim at the validational standards of scientific knowledge but rather seeks to tease out inventive practices (that later may, or may not, be validated as knowledge claims). See also Holmström, Ketokivi, and Hameri (2009).

12. "Experimentation allows hypotheses to die in our stead" (Karl Popper).

References

Adler, P. S., & Clark, K. B. 1991. Behind the Learning Curve: A Sketch of the Learning Process. *Management Science*, 37(3): 267–281.

Allison, G. 1971. *Essence of Decision: Explaining the Cuban Missile Crisis.* Boston, MA: Little, Brown and Company.

Amabile, T. 1988. A Model of Creativity and Innovation in Organizations. In B. M. Staw & L. L. Cummings (Eds.). *Research in Organizational Behavior*, vol. 10, pp. 123–167. Greenwich, CT: JAI Press.

Amabile, T. 1993. Rethinking Rewards. *Harvard Business Review*, 71(6).

Amabile, T., & Conti, R. 1999. Changes in the Work Environment for Creativity during Downsizing. *Academy of Management Journal*, 42: 630–640.

Anderson, N., Herriott, P., & Hodgkinson, G. P. 2001. The Practitioner-Researcher Divide in Industrial Work and Organization (IWO) Psychology: Where Are We Now, and Where Do We Go from Here? *Journal of Occupational and Organizational Psychology*, 74: 391–411.

Ansoff, H. I. 1988. *The New Corporate Strategy.* New York: John Wiley. (Original work published 1965.)

Appleman, E. M. 2004. Democracy in Action, a non-partisan nonprofit Web site hosted at George Washington University that provides data on both 2000 and 2004 presidential elections (www.gwu.edu/~action/P2004.html).

Argyris, C., & Schon, D. 1974/1992. *Theory in Practice: Increasing Professional Effectiveness.* San Francisco: Jossey-Bass.

Argyris, C., & Schon, D. A. 1978. *Organizational Learning.* Reading, MA: Addison-Wesley.

Arlbjorn, J., Johnson, P., & Johanson, J. 2008. A Survey of Nordic Research in Logistics and Supply Chain Management. In J. Arlbjorn, A. Haldorsson,

M. Jahre, & K. Spens (Eds.). *Northern Lights in Logistics and Supply Chain Management*. Copenhagen: Copenhagen Business School Press.

Ashby, W. R. 1956. *An Introduction to Cybernetics*. London: William Clowes & Sons.

Backstrom, H. 1999. Den krattade manegen: Svensk arbetsorganisatorisk utveckling under tre decennier (Swedish Development in Work Organization Under Three Decades). Dept. of Business Studies. Uppsala: Uppsala University.

Bandura, A. 1977. Self-efficacy: Toward a Unifying Theory of Behavioral Change. *Psychological Review*, 84: 191–215.

Barley, S. R., & Kunda, G. 2001. Bringing Work Back In. *Organization Science*, 12(1): 76–95.

Barr, P. S., Stimpert, J. L., & Huff, A. S. 1992. Cognitive Change, Strategic Action, and Organizational Renewal. *Strategic Management Journal*, 13: 15–36.

Barsade, S. G. 2002. The Ripple Effect: Emotional Contagion and Its Influence on Group Behavior. *Administrative Science Quarterly*, 47: 644–676.

Bartlett, C., & Ghoshal, S. 1999. *The Individualized Corporation: A Fundamentally New Approach to Management*. New York: Harper Business.

Bartunek, J. M., Gordon, J. R., & Weathersby, R. P. 1983. Developing "Complicated" Understanding in Administrators. *The Academy of Management Review*, 8: 273–284.

Beer, M. 2001. Why Management Research Findings Are Unimplementable: An Action Science Perspective. *Reflections*, 2(3): 58–65.

Berger, P., & Luckmann, T. 1966. *The Social Construction of Reality: A Treatise in the Sociology of Knowledge*. New York: Doubleday, Anchor.

Birkinshaw, J., Hamel, G., & Mol, M. 2005. Management Innovation. AIM working paper WP–021; www.aimresearch.org/021wp.html.

Blonder, G. 2005. Greg Blonder bio, www.genuineideas.com/GEBBio/geb-bio.html. Last references July 12, 2005.

Boland, R., Jr., & Collopy, F. (Eds.). 2004. *Managing as Designing*. Palo Alto, CA: Stanford University Press.

Bonvillian, W. 2007. The Once and Future Darpa. In F. Fukuyama (Ed.). *Blindside: How to Anticipate Forcing Events and Wild Cards in Global Politics*. Washington, DC: Brookings Institution Press.

Bossidy, L., Charam, R., & Burck, C. 2002. *Execution: The Discipline of Getting Things Done*. New York: Crown Business.

Bower, J. L., & Gilbert, C. G. 2007. How Managers' Everyday Decisions Create or Destroy Your Company's Strategy. *Harvard Business Review*, February: 72–79.

Bowie, N., & Freeman, R. 1992. *Ethics and Agency Theory*. New York: Oxford University Press.

Brockner, J. 1992. The Escalation of Commitment to a Failing Course of Action: Toward Theoretical Progress. *The Academy of Management Review*, 17(1): 39–61.

Brunsson, N. 1996. Managing Organizational Disorder. In M. Warglien & M. Masuch (Eds.). *The Logic of Organizational Disorder*. Berlin: De Gruyter.

Burgelman, R. 1983. Corporate Entrepreneurship and Strategic Management: Inside a Process Study. *Management Science*, December: 193–214.

Burgelman, R., & Välikangas, L. 2005. Managing Internal Venturing Cycles: A Nagging Leadership Challenge. *MIT Sloan Management Review*, Summer: 26–34.

Campbell-Hunt, C. 2000. What Have We Learned about Generic Competitive Strategy? A Meta-Analysis. *Strategic Management Journal*, 21(2): 127–154.

Cattani, G., Pennings, J. M., & Wezel, F. C. 2003. Spatial and Temporal Heterogeneity in Founding Patterns. *Organization Science*, 14(6): 670–685.

Chamberlin, T. C. 1890. The Method of Multiple Working Hypotheses. *Science* (old series), 15: 92–96; reprinted 1965, 148: 754–759.

Chamberlin, T. C. 1897. The Method of Multiple Working Hypotheses. *Journal of Geology*, 5: 837–848.

Chriss, J. J. 1995. Habermas, Goffman, and Communicative Action: Implications for Professional Practice. *American Sociological Review*, 60(4): 545–565.

Christensen, C. 1997. *The Innovator's Dilemma: When New Technologies Cause Great Firms to Fail*. Boston, MA: Harvard Business Press.

Clark, A. W. 1976. *Experimenting with Organizational Life: The Action Research Approach*. New York: Plenum Press.

Clark, A. 1980. Action Research: Theory, Practice and Values. *Journal of Occupational Behavior*, 1(2): 151–157.

Collins, D. 1997. The Ethical Superiority of Participatory Management as an Organizational System. *Organization Science*, 8(5): 489–507.

Collins, J. 2001. *Good to Great: Why Some Companies Make the Leap . . . and Others Don't.* New York: Harper Business.

Collins, J. 2009. *How the Mighty Fall: And Why Some Companies Never Give In.* Jim Collins.

Comm, J. 2009. *Twitter Power: How to Dominate Your Market One Tweet at a Time.* Hoboken, NJ: Wiley.

Conell, C., & Voss, K. 1990. Formal Organization and the Fate of Social Movements: Craft Association and Class Alliance in the Knights of Labor. *American Sociological Review*, 55(2): 255–269.

Cook, S. D. N., & Brown, J. S. 1999. Bridging Epistemologies: The Generative Dance between Organizational Knowledge and Organizational Knowing. *Organization Science*, 10(4): 381–400.

Cyert, R., & March, J. G. 1963. *A Behavioral Theory of the Firm.* Malden, MA: Blackwell Publishers.

Czarniawska, B., & Joerges, B. 1996. Travel of Ideas. In B. Czarniawska & G. Sevon (Eds.). *Translating Organizational Change.* Berlin, New York: Walter de Gruyter.

Czarniawska, B., & Sevón, G. (Eds.). 2005. *Global Ideas: How Ideas, Objects, and Practices Travel in the Global Economy.* Malmö, Sweden: Liber.

D'Aveni, R., & MacMillan, I. 1990. Crisis and the Content of Managerial Communications: A Study of the Focus of Attention of Top Managers in Surviving and Failing Firms. *Administrative Science Quarterly*, 25: 634–665.

Dawkins, R. 1976/2006. *The Selfish Gene* (3rd ed.). Oxford, UK: Oxford University Press.

Dean, H., & Warner, J. 2004. *You Have the Power: How to Take Back Our Country and Restore Democracy in America.* New York: Simon & Schuster.

Denrell, J. 2005. Selection and the Perils of Benchmarking. *Harvard Business Review*, April: 114–120.

Dewar, R. D., & Dutton, J. E. 1986. The Adoption of Radical and Incremental Innovations: An Empirical Analysis. *Management Science*, 32: 1422–1433.

Dhillon, N., & Yousef, T. (Eds.). 2009. *Generation in Waiting*. Washington, DC: Brookings Institution Press.

Diamond, J. 2004. *Collapse: How Societies Choose to Fail or Succeed*. New York: Viking Adult.

DiMaggio, P. J. 1988. Interest and Agency in Institutional Theory. In L. G. Zucker (Ed.). *Institutional Patterns and Organizations: Culture and Environment* (pp. 3–21). Cambridge, MA: Ballinger.

Doz, Y., & Kosonen, M. 2008. *Fast Strategy: How Strategic Agility Will Help You Stay Ahead of the Game*. Philadelphia, PA: Wharton School Publishing.

Dunbar, R. L., & Starbuck, W. H. 2006. Learning to Design Organizations and Learning from Designing Them, Introduction to Special Issue on Organization Design. *Organization Science*, 17(2): 171–178.

Dyson, F. J. 2002. In Praise of Amateurs. *The New York Review of Books,* 49(19): 4–8.

Ellis, C. 2008. *The Partnership: The Making of Goldman Sachs*. New York: Penguin Press.

Ferguson, N. 2009. The Descent of Finance. *Harvard Business Review*, July–August: 44–53.

Fligstein, N. 1997. Social Skill and Institutional Theory. *American Behavioral Scientist*, 40(4): 397–402.

Fligstein, N. 2001. *The Architecture of Markets: An Economic Sociology of Twenty-First-Century Capitalism*. Princeton, NJ: Princeton University Press.

Fligstein, N., & Mara-Drita, I. 1996. How to Make a Market: Reflections on the Attempt to Create a Single Market in the European Union. *American Journal of Sociology*, 102(1): 1–33.

Frank, R. 1988. *Passion within Reason: The Strategic Role of Emotions*. New York: Norton.

Fukuyama, F. 1992. *End of History and the Last Man*. New York: Free Press.

Fukuyama, F. 1995. *Trust: The Social Virtues and the Creation of Prosperity*. New York: Free Press.

Fukuyama, F. (Ed.). 2007. *Blindside: How to Anticipate Forcing Events and Wild Cards in Global Politics*. Washington, DC: Brookings Institution Press.

Futuyama, D. J. 2005. *Evolution*. Sunderland, MA: Sinauer Associates.

Ghoshal, S., & Moran, P. 1996. Bad for Practice: A Critique of the Transaction Cost Theory. *The Academy of Management Review*, 21(1): 13–47.

Gibbert, M., Hoegl, M., & Välikangas, L. 2007. In Praise of Resource Constraints. *MIT Sloan Management Review*, 48(3): 14–17.

Gibbert, M., Välikangas, L., & Hoegl, M. 2009. How Resource Constraints Spark Creativity. Blog. *MIT Sloan Management Review* (April 8), The Downturn Manifesto.

Gilfillan, S. C. 1945. Invention as a Factor in Economic History. *The Journal of Economic History*, 5(Supplement: The Tasks of Economic History): 66–85.

Gist, M. E. 1987. Self-Efficacy: Implications for Organizational Behavior and Human Resource Management. *Academy of Management Review*, 12(3): 472–485.

Gladwell, M. 2008. *Outliers: The Story of Success*. New York: Little, Brown and Company.

Glynn, M. A. 1996. Innovative Genius: A Framework for Relating Individual and Organizational Intelligences to Innovation. *The Academy of Management Review*, 21(4): 1081–1111.

Gourville, J. T. 2006. Eager Sellers, Stony Buyers. *Harvard Business Review*, June: 98–106.

Grant, R. M. 2003. Strategic Planning in a Turbulent Environment: Evidence from the Oil Majors. *Strategic Management Journal*, 24: 491–517.

Greenberger, D. B., & Strasser, S. 1986. Development and Application of a Model of Personal Control in Organizations. *The Academy of Management Review*, 11: 164–178.

Griffin, R., & Kacmar, M. 1991. Laboratory Research in Management: Misconceptions and Missed Opportunities. *Journal of Organizational Behavior*, 12(4): 301–311.

Hagel, J., Brown, J., & Davison, L. 2009. The Big Shift: Measuring the Forces of Change. *Harvard Business Review*, July–August: 44–53.

Hall, G., & Howell, S. 1985. The Experience Curve from the Economist's Perspective. *Strategic Management Journal*, 6(3): 197–212.

Hamel, G. 1999. Bringing Silicon Valley Inside. *Harvard Business Review*, September–October: 70–86.

Hamel, G. 2002. *Leading the Revolution*. Boston, MA: Harvard Business School Press.

Hamel, G., & Breen, B. 2007. *The Future of Management*. Boston, MA: Harvard Business School Press.

Hamel, G., & Välikangas, L. 2003. The Quest for Resilience. *Harvard Business Review*, September: 52–63.

Hänninen, H. I. 2007. Negotiated Risks—The Estonia Accident and the Stream of Bow Visor Failures in the Baltic Ferry Traffic (Doctoral thesis ed.). Helsinki: Helsinki School of Economics. A-300.

Hanson, N. R. 1960. More on the "Logic of Discovery." *The Journal of Philosophy*, 57(6): 182–188.

Hanson, N. R. 1967. The Anatomy of Discovery. *Journal of Philosophy*, 64(11): 321–352.

Hanson, N. R. 1972. *Patterns of Discovery*. Cambridge, UK: Cambridge University Press.

Hatch, M. J. 1997. Irony and the Social Construction of Contradiction in the Humor of a Management Team. *Organization Science*, 8(3): 275–288.

Hedberg, B. L. T., Nystrom, P. C., & Starbuck, W. H. 1976. Camping on Seesaws: Prescriptions for a Self-Designing Organization. *Administrative Science Quarterly*, March 21: 41–65.

Hickman, L. 1990. *John Dewey's Pragmatic Technology*. Bloomington: Indiana University Press.

Hoegl, M., & Gemuenden, H. G. 2001. Teamwork Quality and the Success of Innovative Projects: A Theoretical Concept and Empirical Evidence. *Organization Science*, 12: 435–449.

Hoegl, M., Gibbert, M., & Mazursky, D. 2008. Financial Constraints in Innovation Projects: When Is Less More? *Research Policy*, 37: 1382–1391.

Hoffman, A. J., & Ocasio, W. 2001. Not All Events Are Attended Equally: Toward a Middle-Range Theory of Industry Attention to External Events. *Organization Science*, 12(4): 414–434.

Hogan, E. A. 1987. Effects of Prior Expectations on Performance Ratings: A Longitudinal Study. *The Academy of Management Journal*, 30: 354–368.

Hollnagel, E., & Woods, D. 2006. Epilogue: Resilience Engineering Precepts. In E. Hollnagel, D. Woods, & N. Leveson (Eds.). *Resilience Engineering: Concepts and Precepts*. Hampshire, England: Ashgate.

Hollnagel, E., Woods, D., & Leveson, N. 2006. *Resilience Engineering: Concepts and Precepts*. Hampshire, England: Ashgate.

Holmström, J., Ketokivi, M., & Hameri, A-P. 2009. Bridging Practice and Theory: A Design Science Approach. *Decision Sciences*, 40(1): 65–87.

Howard, R. A. 1970. Management Science Education: Nature and Nurture. *Management Science*, 17(2): B23–B24. Application Series, Educational Issues in the Management Sciences and Operational Research.

Huntington, S. 1996. *The Clash of Civilizations and the Remaking of World Order*. New York: Touchstone.

Huy, Q. N. 1999. Emotional Capability, Emotional Intelligence, and Radical Change. *The Academy of Management Review*, 24(2): 325–346.

Iacovini, J. 1993. The Human Side of Organisational Change. *Training and Development*, 47: 65–69.

Jacobs, J. 1993. *The Death and Life of Great American Cities* (reissue ed.). New York: Random House.

Jett, Q., & Välikangas, L. 2006. "Toward Open-Sourced Design: Digital Media and the Potential for Organizations to Evolve." Presented at the Academy of Management, August.

Johansson, F. 2004. *The Medici Effect: Breakthrough Insights at the Intersection of Ideas, Concepts, and Cultures*. Boston: Harvard Business School Press.

Kahn, W. 2003. The Revelation of Organizational Trauma. *The Journal of Applied Behavioral Science*, 39: 364–380.

Kahneman, D., & Tversky, A. 1979. Prospect Theory: An Analysis of Decision under Risk. *Econometrica*, 47(2): 263–291.

Kaplan, S. 2004. Framing the Future: Cognitive Frames, Strategic Choice, and Firm Response to the Fiber-Optic Revolution, MIT, Ph.D. Dissertation.

Kaplan, S. 2008. Framing Contests: Strategy Making under Uncertainty. *Organization Science*, 19(5): 729–752.

Keats, B. W. 1991. An Empirical Investigation of Strategic Investment Decision Models. *Strategic Management Journal*, 12(3): 243–250.

Kets de Vries, M. F. R. 1990. The Organizational Fool: Balancing a Leader's Hubris. *Human Relations*, 43(8): 751.

Kets de Vries, M. F. R. 2003. *Leaders, Fools and Imposters: Essays on the Psychology of Leadership* (rev. ed.). Lincoln, NE: iUniverse, Inc.

Kim, C. W., & Mauborgne, R. 2005. *Blue Ocean Strategy: How to Create Uncontested Market Space and Make Competition Irrelevant.* Boston: Harvard Business Press.

Klapp, O. E. 1949. The Fool as a Social Type. *The American Journal of Sociology*, 55(2): 157–162.

Klapp, O. E. 1962. *Heroes, Villains, and Fools: The Changing American Character.* Englewood Cliffs, NJ: Prentice Hall.

Kleiner, A. 1996. *The Age of Heretics.* New York: Currency/Doubleday.

Kleiner, A. 2003. *Who Really Matters: The Core Group Theory of Power, Privilege, and Success.* New York: Currency/Doubleday.

Knights, D. 1992. Changing Spaces: The Disruptive Impact of a New Epistemological Paradigm for the Study of Management. *Academy of Management Review*, 17(3): 514–536.

Koestler, A. 1967. *The Act of Creation: A Study of Conscious and Unconscious in Science and Art.* New York: Dell Publishing.

Lau, R. R., & Redlawsk, D. P. 2001. Advantages and Disadvantages of Cognitive Heuristics in Political Decision Making. *American Journal of Political Science*, 45(4): 951–971.

Levchuk, G., Meirina, C., Levchuk, Y., Pattipati, K., & Kleiman, D. 2001. Design and Analysis of Robust and Adaptive Organizations. June–July 2001 Command and Control Research and Technology Symposium (A2C2 session), Annapolis, MD.

Levinthal, D. A., & March, J. G. 1993. The Myopia of Learning. *Strategic Management Journal*, 14 (special issue: Organizations, Decision Making, and Strategy): 95–112.

Levitt, B., & March, J. G. 1988. Organizational Learning. *Annual Review of Sociology*, 14: 319–340.

Lewin, A. Y. 1989. On Learning from Outliers. In W. W. Cooper (Ed.). *Developments in Management Science: A Volume in Honor of Abraham Charnes on His 70th Birthday.* Bollinger.

Lewin, K. 1945. The Research Center for Group Dynamics at Massachusetts Institute of Technology. *Sociometry*, 8(2): 126–136.

Liddel Hart, B. H. 1968. *Strategy.* London: Faber & Faber.

Lindblom, C. E. 1987. Alternatives to Validity: Some Thoughts Suggested by Campbell's Guidelines. *Science Communication,* 8: 509–520.

Littwin, M. 2004. Dean's Got Sticking Power; Despite His Blunders, "Pin Cushion" Leads in Polls, Money, and Crowds. *Rocky Mountain News,* January 14: 36A.

Locke, K., & Brazelton, J. K. 1997. Why Do We Ask Them to Write, or Whose Writing Is It, Anyway? *Journal of Management Education,* 21: 44–57.

Lovio, R. 1993. *Evolution of Firm Communities in New Industries: The Case of the Finnish Electronics Industry.* Helsinki, Finland: The Helsinki School of Economics and Business Administration Ph.D. Dissertation.

Luft, G., & Korin, A. 2007. Fueled Again? In Search of Energy Security. In F. Fukuyama (Ed.). *Blindside: How to Anticipate Forcing Events and Wild Cards in Global Politics.* Washington, DC: Brookings Institution Press.

Malone, T. 2004. *The Future of Work: How the New Order of Business Will Shape Your Organization, Your Management Style, and Your Life.* Boston: Harvard Business School Press.

March, J. G. 1978. Bounded Rationality, Ambiguity, and the Engineering of Choice. *Bell Journal of Economics,* 9: 587–608.

March, J. G. 1981. Footnotes to Organizational Change. *Administrative Science Quarterly,* 26(4): 563–577.

March, J. G. 1991. Exploration and Exploitation in Organizational Learning. *Organization Science,* 2(1, Special Issue: Organizational Learning: Papers in Honor of—and by—James G. March): 71–87.

March, J. G., & Olsen, J. P. 1976. *Ambiguity and Choice in Organizations.* Bergen, Norway: Universitetsforlaget.

March, J. G., & Olsen, J. P. 1989. *Rediscovering Institutions: The Organizational Basis of Politics.* New York: Free Press.

March, J. G., & Olsen, J. 1995. *Democratic Governance.* New York: Free Press.

March, J. G., & Shapira, Z. 1987. Managerial Perspectives on Risk and Risk Taking. *Management Science,* 33(11): 1404–1418.

March, J. G., & Simon, H. A. 1958. *Organizations.* New York: Wiley.

March, J. G., Sproull, L., & Tamuz, M. 1991. Learning from Samples of One or Fewer. *Organization Science*, 2(1): 1–13.

Mason, R. O. 1969. A Dialectical Approach to Strategic Planning. *Management Science*, 15(8): B403–B414, Application Series.

Massey, D. S. 2002. A Brief History of Human Society: The Origin and Role of Emotion in Social Life: 2001 Presidential Address. *American Sociological Review*, 67: 1–29.

McAdam, D., & Snow, D. A. 1997. *Social Movements: Readings in Their Emergence, Mobilization, and Dynamics*. Los Angeles: Roxbury.

McClosky, D. N. 1988. The Limits of Expertise. *American Scholar*, 57(3): 393–406.

McGrath, R. G. 1997. A Real Options Logic for Initiating Technology Positioning Investments. *The Academy of Management Review*, 22: 974–996.

McGrath, R. G. 1999. Falling Forward: Real Options Reasoning and Entrepreneurial Failure. *The Academy of Management Review*, 24(1): 13–30.

McKelvey, B. 1997. Quasi-Natural Organization Science. *Organization Science*, 8(4): 352–380.

McLean, B., & Elkind, P. 2003. *Smartest Guys in the Room: The Amazing Rise and Scandalous Fall of Enron*. New York: Portfolio.

Merton, R., & Barber, E. 2004. *The Travels and Adventures of Serendipity: A Study in Sociological Semantics and the Sociology of Science*. Princeton, NJ: Princeton University Press.

Meyer, J. W., & Rowan, B. 1991. Institutionalized Organizations: Formal Structure as Myth and Ceremony. In P. J. DiMaggio & W. W. Powell (Eds.). *The New Institutionalism in Organizations* (pp. 108–140). Chicago: University of Chicago Press. (Original work published in 1977.)

Meyer, M., & Zucker, L. 1989. *Permanently Failing Organizations*. Newbury Park, CA: Sage.

Meyerson, D. 2001. *Tempered Radicals: How People Use Difference to Inspire Change at Work*. Boston: Harvard Business School Press.

Mezias, J. M., & Starbuck, W. H. 2003. Studying the Accuracy of Managers' Perceptions: A Research Odyssey. *British Journal of Management*, 14: 3–17.

Miller, D. 1990. *The Icarus Paradox: How Exceptional Companies Bring About Their Own Downfall.* New York: Harper Business.

Miller, D. 1993. The Architecture of Simplicity. *Academy of Management Review,* 18(1): 116–138.

Miller, D., & Chen, M-J. 1994. Sources and Consequences of Competitive Inertia: A Study of the U.S. Airline Industry. *Administrative Science Quarterly,* 39(1): 1–23.

Miner, A. S., & Mezias, S. J. 1996. Ugly Duckling No More: Pasts and Futures of Organizational Learning Research. *Organization Science,* 7(1): 88–99.

Mintzberg, H. 1979. An Emerging Strategy of "Direct" Research. *Administrative Science Quarterly,* 24(4): 582–589.

Mintzberg, H. 1990. The Design School: Reconsidering Basic Premises of Strategic Management. *Strategic Management Journal,* 11(3): 171–195.

Mintzberg, H. 1994. *The Rise and Fall of Strategic Planning.* New York: Free Press.

Mintzberg, H., & Waters, J. A. 1985. Of Strategies, Deliberate and Emergent. *Strategic Management Journal,* 6(3): 257–272.

Moldenhauer-Salazar, J., & Välikangas, L. 2008. Sun Ray's Struggle to Overcome Innovation Trauma. *Strategy & Leadership,* Summer: 15–20.

Moore, G. A. 1991. *Crossing the Chasm.* New York: Harper Business.

Muller, A., & Välikangas, L. 2003. An "ODD" Reaction to Strategy Failure in America's (Once) Largest Telco. *European Management Journal,* 21(1): 109–119.

Nadler, D. A. 1988. Concepts for the Management of Organizational Change. In M. L. Tushman & W. L. Moore (Eds.). *Readings in the Management of Innovations* (pp. 718–731). Cambridge, MA: Ballinger Publishing Company.

Newell, A., & Simon, H. A. 1972. *Human Problem Solving.* Englewood Cliffs, NJ: Prentice-Hall.

North, D. C. 1990. Institutions, Institutional Change, and Economic Performance. In J. Alt & D. North (Series Eds.). *Political Economy of Institutions and Decisions.* Cambridge, UK: Cambridge University Press.

North, D. C., & Weingast, B. M. 1989. Constitutions and Commitment: The Evolution of Institutions Governing Public Choice in Seventeenth-Century England. *Economic History,* 49(4): 803–832.

Oakes, L., Townley, B., & Cooper, D. 1998. Business Planning as Pedagogy: Languages and Control in a Changing Institutional Field. *Administrative Science Quarterly*, 43(2), Special Issue: Critical Perspectives on Organizational Control: 257–292.

Ocasio, W. 1997. Towards an Attention-Based View of the Firm. *Strategic Management Journal*, 18(Summer 1997) Special Issue: Organizational and Competitive Interactions: 187–206.

Oliver, C. 1997. Sustainable Competitive Advantage: Combining Institutional and Resource-Based Views. *Strategic Management Journal*, 18(9): 697–713.

Olivera, J. 1971. The Square-Root Law of Precautionary Reserves. *The Journal of Political Economy*, 79(5): 1095–1104.

Önkal, D., Yates, J. F., Simga-Mugan, C., & Öztin, S. 2003. Professional vs. Amateur Judgment Accuracy: The Case of Foreign Exchange Rates. *Organizational Behavior and Human Decision Processes*, 91(2): 169–185.

Otto, B. K. 2001. *Fools Are Everywhere: The Court Jester around the World*. Illinois: University of Chicago Press.

Padgett, J., & Ansell, C. 1993. Robust Action and the Rise of the Medici, 1400–1434. *The American Journal of Sociology*, 98(6): 1259–1319.

Pascale, R. 1984. Perspectives on Strategy: The Real Story behind Honda's Success. *California Management Review*, XXVI(3): 47–72.

Pascale, R. 1996. Reflections on Honda. *California Management Review*, 38(4): 112–117.

Perrow, C. 1984. *Normal Accidents*. New York: Basic Books.

Perrow, C. 1986. *Complex Organizations: A Critical Essay* (3rd ed.). New York: McGraw-Hill.

Pfeffer, J., & Fong, C. 2005. Building Organization Theory from First Principles: The Self-Enhancement Motive and Understanding of Power and Influence. *Organization Science*, 16(4): 372–388.

Pfeffer, J., & Salancik, G. 1978. *The External Control of Organizations: A Resource Dependence Perspective*. New York: Harper & Row.

Piven, F. F., & Cloward, R. A. 1979. *Poor People's Movements: Why They Succeed, How They Fail*. New York: Vintage.

Platt, J. R. 1964. Strong Inference. *Science*, 146(3642): 347– 353.

Polimeni, J., & Reiss, J. P. 2006. The First Joke: Exploring the Evolutionary Origins of Humor. *Evolutionary Psychology*, 4: 347–366.

Porter, M. E. 1980. *Competitive Strategy*. New York: Free Press.

Postrel, V. 1998. *The Future and Its Enemies*. New York: Free Press.

Prahalad, C. K. 2004. *The Fortune at the Bottom of the Pyramid: Eradicating Poverty through Profits*. Philadelphia, PA: Wharton School Publishing.

Probst, G. 2002. Putting Knowledge to Work: Case Writing as an Organizational Learning and Knowledge Management Tool for the New Economy. In G. Probst & T. H. Davenport (Eds.). *Knowledge Management Case Book* (pp. 248–261). Erlangen, Germany: Publicis and Wiley.

Raelin, J. A. 1997. A Model of Work-Based Learning. *Organization Science*, 8(6): 563–578.

Ramachandran, V. S. 1998. The Neurology and Evolution of Humor, Laughter, and Smiling: The False Alarm Theory. *Medical Hypotheses*, 51: 351–354.

Rao, H. 2009. *Market Rebels: How Activists Make or Break Radical Innovations*. New Jersey: Princeton University Press.

Rindova, V. P., & Kotha, S. 2001. Continuous "Morphing": Competing through Dynamic Capabilities, Form, and Function. *Academy of Management Journal*, 44(6): 1263–1280.

Rogers, E. M. 1995. *Diffusion of Innovation* (4th ed.). New York: Free Press.

Romme, A. G. L. 2003. Making a Difference: Organization as Design. *Organization Science*, 14(5): 558–573.

Ross, J., & Staw, B. M. 1993. Organizational Escalation and Exit: Lessons from the Shoreham Nuclear Power Plant. *The Academy of Management Journal*, 36(4): 701–732.

Rynes, S., Bartunek, J., & Daft, R. 2001. Across the Great Divide: Knowledge Creation and Transfer between Practitioners and Academics. *Academy of Management Journal*, 44(2): 340–355.

Schnarrs, S. P. 1988. *Mega Mistakes: Forecasting and the Myth of Radical Technological Change*. New York: Free Press.

Schwartz, P., & Randall, D. 2007. Ahead of the Curve: Anticipating Strategic Surprise. In F. Fukuyama (Ed.). *Blindside: How to Anticipate*

Forcing Events and Wild Cards in Global Politics. Washington, DC: Brookings Institution Press.

Scott, W. R. 1994. Institutions and Organizations: Towards a Theoretical Synthesis. In W. R. Scott & J. W. Meyer (Eds.). *Institutional Environments and Organizations.* Newbury Park, CA: Sage.

Scott, W. R. 2001. *Institutions and Organizations: Foundations for Organizational Science.* Newbury Park, CA: Sage. (Original work published in 1995.)

Scott, W. R., & Meyer, J. W. 1991. The Organization of Societal Sectors: Propositions and Early Evidence. In P. J. DiMaggio & W. W. Powell (Eds.). *The New Institutionalism in Organizations* (pp. 108–140). Chicago: University of Chicago Press. (Original work published in 1983.)

Sevon, G., & Välikangas, L. 2009. Of Managers, Ideas, and Jesters, SSE/EFI Working Paper Series in Business Administration, No. 2009:1, Stockholm School of Economics, Sweden.

Shepsle, K. A., & Bonchek, M. S. 1997. *Analyzing Politics: Rationality, Behavior, and Institutions.* New York: W.W. Norton.

Simon, H. A. 1947. *Administrative Behavior: A Study of Decision-Making Processes in Administrative Organizations.* New York: Macmillan.

Simon, H. A. 1979. Rational Decision Making in Business Organizations. *The American Economic Review,* 69(4): 493–513.

Starbuck, W. H. 2006. *The Production of Knowledge.* Oxford, UK: Oxford University Press.

Starr, J., & MacMillan, I. 1990. Resource Cooptation via Social Contracting: Resource Acquisition Strategies for New Ventures. *Strategic Management Journal,* 11(4): 79–92.

Staw, B. M., & Ross, J. 1987. Behavior in Escalation Situations: Antecedents, Prototypes, and Solutions. *Research in Organizational Behavior,* 9: 39–78.

Stuart, R. 1996. The Trauma of Organizational Change. *Journal of European Industrial Training,* 20: 11–16.

Sull, D. 1999. Why Good Companies Go Bad. *Harvard Business Review,* July–August: 2–10.

Sull, D. 2005. *Made in China: What Western Managers Can Learn from Trailblazing Chinese Entrepreneurs.* Boston: Harvard Business Press.

Szulanski, G. 2003. *Sticky Knowledge: Barriers to Knowing in the Firm.* Newbury Park, CA: Sage.

Taguchi, G. 1986. *Introduction to Quality Engineering.* White Plains, NY: UNIPUB/Krauss International.

Taguchi, G. 1987. *System of Experimental Design,* vols. 1 and 2. White Plains, NY: UNIPUB/Krauss International.

Taleb, N. 2007. *The Black Swan: The Impact of the Highly Improbable.* New York: Random House.

Thaler, R. H., Tversky, A., Kahneman, D., & Schwartz, A. 1997. The Effect of Myopia and Loss Aversion on Risk Taking: An Experimental Test. *The Quarterly Journal of Economics,* 112(2) in Memory of Amos Tversky (1937–1996): 647–661.

Thomas, A. S. 1998. The Business Policy Course: Multiple Methods for Multiple Goals. *Journal of Management Education,* 22: 484–497.

Thomke, S. 1998. Managing Experimentation in the Design of New Products. *Management Science,* 44(6): 743–762.

Tolbert, P. S., & Zucker, L. G. 1996. Institutionalization of Institutional Theory. In S. Clegg, C. Hardy, & W. Nord (Eds.). *Handbook of Organization Studies* (pp. 175–190). London: Sage.

Triana, P. 2008. *Lecturing Birds on Flying: Can Mathematical Theories Destroy the Financial Markets?* Hoboken, NJ: Wiley.

Trippi, J. 2004. *The Revolution Will Not Be Televised.* New York: HarperCollins.

Tripsas, M., & Giovanni, G. 2000. Capabilities and Inertia: Evidence from Digital Imaging. *Strategic Management Journal,* 21(10–11): 1147–1161.

Tuomi, I. 2003. *Networks of Innovation: Change and Meaning in the Age of the Internet.* Oxford, UK: Oxford University Press.

Tversky, A., & Kahneman, D. 1986. Rational Choice and the Framing of Decisions. *The Journal of Business,* 59(4) Part 2: The Behavioral Foundations of Economic Theory: S251–S278.

Uglow, J. 2002. *The Lunar Men: Five Friends Whose Curiosity Changed the World.* New York: Farrar, Straus and Giroux.

Välikangas, L. (2007/2008). The Challenge of Inventive Experimentation to Management Research, as a Woodside Institute Working Paper,

Woodside, CA, in 2006 and presented to the Organization Science Winter Conference in February 2007 and to the Academy of Management in August 2008.

Välikangas, L., & Gibbert, M. 2005. Boundary-Setting Strategies for Escaping Innovation Traps. *MIT Sloan Management Review*, 46(3): 57–65.

Välikangas, L., & Gibbert, M. 2008. When Less Is More. *Stanford Social Innovation Review*, Summer: 27.

Välikangas, L., Hoegl, M., & Gibbert, M. 2009. Why Learning from Failure Isn't Easy (and What to Do about It): Innovation Trauma at Sun Microsystems. *European Management Journal*, 27(4): 225–233.

Välikangas, L., & Jett, Q. 2006. The Golden Spur: Innovation Independence. *Strategy & Leadership*, 34(5): 41–45.

Van de Ven, A. H., & Johnson, P. E. 2006. Knowledge for Theory and Practice. *Academy of Management Review*, 31: 802–821.

Vaughan, D. 1996. *The Challenger Launch Decision: Risky Technology, Culture, and Deviance at NASA*. Chicago: University of Chicago Press.

Von Hippel, E. 2005. *Democratizing Innovation*. Boston, MA: MIT Press.

Von Krogh, G. 2003. Open-Source Software Development. *MIT Sloan Management Review*, 44(3): 14–18.

Warglien, M., & Masuch, M. (Eds.). 1996. *The Logic of Organizational Disorder*. Berlin: De Gruyter.

Warner, M. 1984. *Organizations and Experiments*. New York: Wiley.

Weick, K. E. 1976. Educational Organizations as Loosely Coupled Systems. *Administrative Science Quarterly*, 21: 1–19.

Weick, K. E. 1988. Enacted Sensemaking in Crisis Situations. *Journal of Management Studies*, 25: 305–318.

Weick, K. E. 1989. Theory Construction as Disciplined Imagination. *Academy of Management Review*, 14(4): 516–531.

Weick, K. E. 1991. The Nontraditional Quality of Organizational Learning. *Organization Science*, 2(1): 116–124. Special Issue: Organizational Learning: Papers in Honor of (and by) James G. March.

Weick, K. E. 1996. Drop Your Tools: An Allegory for Organizational Studies. *Administrative Science Quarterly*, 41(2) 40th Anniversary Issue: 301–313.

Weick, K. E. 2000. *Making Sense of Organizations*. Malden, MA: Blackwell.

Weick, K. E., & Quinn, R. 1999. Organizational Change and Development. *Annual Review of Psychology*, 50(1): 361–387.

Weick, K. E., & Sutcliffe, K. 2001. *Managing the Unexpected: Assuring High Performance in an Age of Complexity*. San Francisco: Jossey-Bass.

Weick, K. E., & Sutcliffe, K. 2007. *Managing the Unexpected: Resilient Performance in an Age of Uncertainty*. San Francisco: Jossey-Bass.

Weiss, C. H. 2000. The Experimentation Society in a Political World. In L. Buckman (Ed.). *Validity and Social Experimentation*. Newbury Park, CA: Sage.

Westman, M., & Etzion, D. 1995. Crossover of Stress, Strain, and Resources from One Spouse to Another. *Journal of Organizational Behavior*, 16(2): 169–181.

Whittington, R. 2002. Seeing Strategy as Social Practice, Key Note Presentation, University of Umea, Sweden, May 5–7.

Whyte, G., Saks, A. M., & Hook, S. 1997. When Success Breeds Failure: The Role of Self-Efficacy in Escalating Commitment to a Losing Course of Action. *Journal of Organizational Behavior*, 18(5): 415–432.

Wiener, N. 1993. *Invention: The Care and Feeding of Ideas*. Boston, MA: MIT Press.

Willeford, W. 1969. *The Fool and His Scepter: A Study in Clowns and Jesters and Their Audience*. Evanston, IL: Northwestern University Press.

Williamson, O. 2000. New Institutional Economics: Taking Stock, Looking Ahead. *Journal of Economic Literature*, 38(September): 595–613.

Winchester, S. 1998. *The Professor and the Madman: A Tale of Murder, Insanity, and the Making of the Oxford English Dictionary*. New York: First Harper Perennial.

Winchester, S. 2003. *The Meaning of Everything: The Story of the Oxford English Dictionary*. Oxford, UK: Oxford University Press.

Witteloostuijn, A. 1998. Bridging Behavioral and Economic Theories of Decline: Organizational Inertia, Strategic Competition, and Chronic Failure. *Management Science*, 44(4): 501–519.

Wood, R. C., Hatten, K. J., & Williamson, P. 2004. The Emergence of Continual Strategic Innovation. San Jose State University Department of Organization and Management Working Paper No. 051E.

Wood, R., & Välikangas, L. 2008. Managers Who Can Transform Institutions in Their Firms: Activism and Practices That Stick. In D. Barry & H. Hansen (Eds.). *Sage Handbook of New and Emerging Approaches to Management & Organization*. Newbury Park, CA: Sage.

Index

About the Author

Dr. Liisa Välikangas is professor of innovation management at the the Aalto University School of Economics (formerly Helsinki School of Economics) in Finland. She is the cofounder and president of Innovation Democracy, a nonprofit global organization dedicated to supporting local innovation and entrepreneurship. Her research on innovation, strategy, and organization has been published in *Harvard Business Review*, *MIT/Sloan Management Review*, and *The Wall Street Journal*. With Gary Hamel, she coauthored the *Harvard Business Review* article "The Quest for Resilience" and cofounded the Woodside Institute, a research organization dedicated to advancing management innovation. Professor Välikangas currently divides her time between Helsinki and California.